PRO/AM
GUIDE TO GOLF

MAPLEWOOD, NEW JERSEY 07040

Much of the material in PRO-AM GUIDE TO GOLF is based upon *Golf Guide*, compiled and edited by Joseph Gambatese and published by Hammond Incorporated © Copyright 1981. Mr. Gambatese is a member of the Golf Writers Association of America.

Library of Congress Cataloging in Publication Data

Main entry under title:

Pro-am guide to golf.

1. Golf.   I. Hammond Incorporated.
GV965.P75   796.352'3   82-2904
ISBN 0-8437-4413-8   AACR2

CONTENTS

INTRODUCTION

If racing is the sport of kings, golf was long the sport of wealthy gentlemen and ardent Scotsmen. No longer—now anyone can play.

The ever-increasing popularity of golf has brought it from what was at the turn of the century, a diversion for the wealthy and the elite, to a sport that, in the United States alone, is played by about 11 million men, women and children who tee off at least 15 times a year. Construction of public courses has literally opened up the game to all. By the mid-'70's public courses outnumbered private courses by almost 2,000 and are used today by more than 84 percent of American golfers.

Women married to keen golfers once were classified as "golf widows," but they are widows no longer. "If you can't beat 'em, join 'em" does not apply here, since women not only have joined 'em but sometimes are beating 'em as well. About one and a half million children are busy perfecting their strokes, and their numbers are increasing every year.

Traditionally, Scotland has been considered the birthplace of golf, which was supposedly invented by a lonesome shepherd who whiled away the empty hours by hitting at round stones with his staff. Earlier forms of the game, such as paganica (played by Romans) and kolven (played by the Dutch), are known to have been played throughout the world, but Scotland is the place where the game was first recorded and where the first "modern" golf course was constructed (at Leith in 1744).

By the 15th century, the game was so popular in Scotland that even the archers were neglecting their compulsory archery practice to hit the ball (then probably a rounded piece of wood) over the turf, and in 1457 the Scottish parliament enacted laws to ban the game for the sake of national defense. But the Scots remained avid golfers, forcing parliament to rewrite laws banning the game throughout the 15th and 16th centuries until 1592, when they came up with a watered-down version prohibiting the playing of golf only on the Sabbath.

All attempts to ban golf were abandoned after one Sunday in the early 1600's when messengers carried the news of the Irish rebellion to the Links of Leith where contrary to law, their monarch, King Charles I, was playing a round.

Early records indicate that golf was played in America by Scottish officers of the British army during the Revolution. The first organized golf club was established in the United States in 1888 at Yonkers, N.Y., and the first public course was constructed in 1896 in Franklin Park, Boston.

Today's most dedicated golfers might become disenchanted with the game if they were subjected to the frustrations of players in early days. The first ball, the kind used by King Charles in his illegal game, was made of feathers wrapped in leather. It often disintegrated on a high drive and scattered its contents through the air.

In 1848, the feather ball was replaced by the "gutta-percha" ball, or "bouncing gilly," which was a solid ball made of resins from Malaysian trees. Since they were lower in price, the "gutties" helped popularize the game. At the turn of the century they were succeeded by a rubber ball made of tightly wound rubber strings wrapped in a hard, dimpled cover.

The mystique of golf and the dedication of the early, somewhat primitive players has carried through to this day. Even the most assured veterans of the links find it difficult to explain their fascination with the sport. And this fascination is shared by others from Lapland to the Netherlands to Mauritius, a remote island far out in the Indian Ocean. Golf is the most widely played outdoor game in the world, and its name is the same in every language—although in the early days the caddie boys at the Royal Hong Kong Club called it "Hittee-Ball-Say-Damn." Rules, etiquette and methods of handicapping and scoring are much the same worldwide.

FUNDAMENTALS AND TECHNIQUE

GRIP

OVERLAPPING

Vardon grip most widely used.

Hold club diagonally in left palm.
Grip firmly with last three fingers.
Place left thumb slightly to
right on shaft.
V formed by thumb and forefinger
points to right shoulder.
Left thumb fits into right palm.

Place right thumb slightly to left.
Little finger of right hand
overlaps left index finger.

Grip of right hand ½ grip of left.
V formed points to right eye.
Hold club firmly, not too tightly.
Hands compactly together.
Maintain firm grip with left hand.

INTERLOCKING

Used by Nicklaus, Sarazen.
Helpful for small hands.

Little finger of right hand
locks with left index finger.

UNLAP

Baseball grip often used by
women beginners. All ten fingers
directly on shaft.

STANCE

WOODS — feet shoulder width apart.

IRONS — feet closer together as loft increases.

Knees flexed slightly.

SQUARE STANCE

Toes on a line parallel to line of flight.

With driver and long irons, ball off left heel (A).

With medium irons, ball closer to center (B).

CLOSED STANCE

Right foot slightly back from line of flight (C).

Sometimes used with driver. Use for intentional hook.

OPEN STANCE

Left foot slightly back from line of flight.

The shorter the distance, the more open the stance. (D).

Use for intentional slice, explosion out of trap.

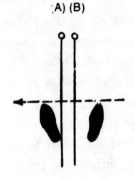

(A) (B)

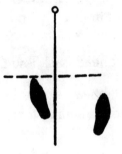

(C)

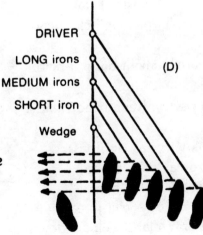

DRIVER
LONG irons
MEDIUM irons
SHORT iron
Wedge

(D)

BACKSWING

Start swing correctly and
you'll likely finish correctly.

Flex knees forward and turn
slightly inward (knock-kneed)
to prevent lateral sway.

Start swing in one piece, hands,
arms and shoulders together
after slight forward press.

Turn left shoulder under chin
and pivot in one flowing movement.

Start clubhead back low to ground.

Swing clubhead slowly but
rhythmically, setting tempo.

Don't cock wrists at start
and don't "pick up" clubhead.

Left arm straight but not rigid.

Don't sway. Keep head steady.

Break wrists as club passes
horizontal, cock at top
with back of left hand
in straight line with forearm,
right arm relaxed, elbow down.

DOWNSWING

Start downswing with pull of
left arm and left side.

Shift weight to left side.

Keep left side firm
and left arm straight.

Delay uncocking wrists until
clubhead reaches hitting zone.

Think of driving butt end
of grip toward ball.

Whip clubhead through ball from
inside line of flight with both hands,
throwing clubhead toward target.

Don't sway, head steady.

Strike ball with
determination, convincingly.

FOLLOW-THROUGH

Hit straight along line toward target.

Extend left arm and keep it straight
as long as possible. This helps
keep clubface on target longer.

Finish with hands high,
facing hole. Weight on left side.

WOODS

THE DRIVER

Approach ball from rear.
Note wind, terrain, obstacles.
Choose best line of direction.

Square or slightly closed
stance, ball off left heel.

Feet shoulder width apart,
knees flexed and inward.

Extended left arm in control.
Firm left hand grip.

Hit square, full follow through.

Hands high at finish.

For extra distance,
play ball more forward.

Open stance will get
left hip out of way
for free body turn.

FAIRWAY WOODS

Square or slightly open stance.

Play ball farther back and
open stance more as you move
down from 2-wood through 5-wood.

Sweep ball off turf.

Avoid over-swinging for
better control.

IRONS

LONG IRONS

Accuracy all important both in direction and distance.

Consider lie, wind, terrain, obstacles, and your ability.

Square stance, ball front of center.

Bottom edge of club square to target.

Start back low, left arm extended, full pivot, long swing

Strike sweeping (not cutting) blow.

Let length of backswing control distance.

MEDIUM IRONS

Open stance very slightly, feet closer together.

Play ball more toward center.

Use shorter backswing as clubs get shorter.

Keep left heel on ground.

Hit down and through ball, taking divot.

PITCHING

PITCH AND STOP

Useful to land and stop ball
near hole up to 90 yards away.

Use 9-iron or pitching wedge.

Open stance, ball in center.

Stand well over ball,
keeping weight on left foot.

Choke down couple inches on grip.

Take three-quarters swing,
strike down on ball
to impart backspin.

Don't scoop. Control distance
by length of backswing.

For accurate direction,
hold club and strike ball with back
of left hand facing target.

PITCH AND RUN

Useful up to 50 yards out and
where there is room on green
for ball to roll.

Use 8-iron or 9-iron.

Land ball on green short
enough of hole for ball to roll.

Allow for contour and grain
of green. Grain against you
will slow roll.

CHIPPING

Useful for delicate shot close to and with clear shot at green.

Select target spot to land ball for roll to pin.

Use less lofted club for short chip.

Medium lofted club for medium chip.

More lofted club for long chip.

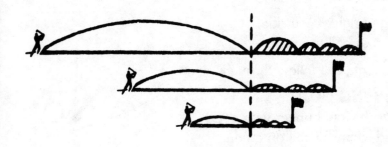

Shorten grip.
Feet closer together.

Open stance.
Knees flexed.

Weight more on left.
Hands ahead of ball, close to body.

Clubface square to line.

Take club back on low arc.

Hit down and follow through along line.

BUNKER SHOTS

EXPLOSION

Feet flat, solidly in sand.

Open stance, open clubface,
hands ahead of clubhead.

Focus and hit one to two
inches behind ball.

Aim to left, use extra wrist,
little body action.

Swing upright to outside,
cut across ball to inside.

Finish high, full follow through.

CHIPPING OUT

Use in shallow bunker with good
lie and room for roll on green.

Open stance, feet close together,
ball off right heel, open
clubface slightly.

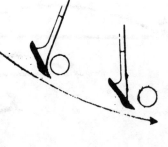

Aim at pin, using wrists mostly,
striking ball before sand.

FAIRWAY BUNKER

Strike ball as you would off fairway,
hitting down and through.

Don't try to help ball out.

PUTTING OUT

Play ball off left heel,
strike crisply, don't touch sand.

WIND SHOTS

Observe trees, flag,
or other players' shots
for direction and force
of wind, or toss pinch
of grass in air.

INTO WIND

Don't hit harder. Use
less lofted club than usual.

Play ball farther back.

Close club face slightly.

Play boldly to pin.

Hit down and through.
Concentrate on making good contact.

WITH WIND

Tee ball higher,
more off left foot.

Play short, run ball to pin.

Avoid pitch shot to pin.

CROSS WIND

Use less lofted club than usual.

Allow for wind to affect
ball's flight.

Aim accordingly to compensate.

SIDEHILL LIES

STANDING ABOVE BALL

Stand nearer to ball,
more weight on heels,
knee flexed.

Lengthen grip.

Longer arc will increase
power. Use one less club.

Ball in center.

Aim slightly left,
(high side).

Heels and body down
throughout swing.

STANDING BELOW BALL

Shorten grip. Shorter arc
will decrease power. Use
one more club.

Open stance, with
more weight on toes.

Aim slightly right,
(high side).

Swing flatter,
straight back.

Hit through straight,
keeping back of left
hand facing target.

TIP TO REMEMBER

Aim to high side.

UPHILL AND DOWNHILL LIES

UPHILL

Use less-lofted club
than normal.

Ball left of center,
(closer to higher foot).

More weight on higher foot.

Shorten swing.

Hit up hill. Aim to right.

DOWNHILL

Use more-lofted club
than normal.

Ball back of center,
(closer to higher foot).

More weight on higher foot.

Shorten swing.

Swing more upright.

Hit down hill. Aim to left.

TIPS TO REMEMBER

Position ball closer
to higher foot.

Let swing follow slope.

SLICING AND HOOKING

CORRECTING SLICE

Turn hands more to right on grip.

Square or closed stance.

Keep right elbow pointing down.

Swing back low and inside. using minimum wrist action.

Clubface square on line of flight.

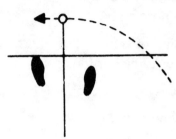

CORRECTING HOOK

Turn hands more to left on grip.

Open stance slightly.

Allow left hand to control and dominate swing.

Use upright swing.

Finish high, hands above head.

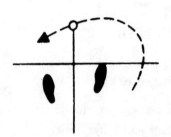

DELIBERATE SLICE

Open stance.

Open clubface slightly.

Swing from outside in, hitting across ball.

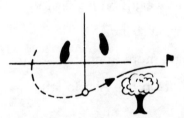

DELIBERATE HOOK

Close stance.

Grip with right hand turned under shaft, with thumbs on right side.

Close clubface slightly. Swing flat, from inside out.

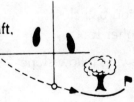

TOPPING AND SKYING

HOW TO STOP TOPPING

Stand closer to ball. Avoid crouch and bent left arm.

Keep head steady. Avoid raising it soo soon, coming off ball. Don't chop.

Keep knees flexed. Don't stiffen knees or shift weight to toes.

Don't try to scoop ball or lean to right at impact. Keep eyes behind ball.

HOW TO STOP SKYING

Skying can result from dropping right shoulder and lowering arc of swing in anxiety to get more power in shot.

Can also cause "fat" shot when iron hits ground behind ball.

On drive, tee ball lower.

Keep head on same level. Don't dip.

Don't break wrists too early or release too soon, causing scoop.

Let left side lead clubhead through ball.

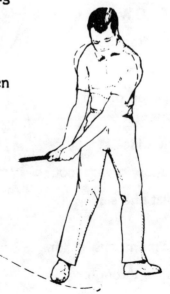

HITTING HIGH AND LOW BALLS

TO HIT A HIGH BALL

Use more lofted club.
Play ball forward.

Open club face slightly.

Hands even with or
behind ball at address.

Swing more upright.

Hit ball down and harder.

Use extra wrist action.

High follow through.

TO HIT LOW BALL

Use less-lofted club.

Play ball back.

Hands ahead of ball
at address.

Close club face slightly.

Weight more on left foot.

Swing flat and stay
down.

Use minimum wrist action.

Low follow through.

SWING CHECKPOINTS

VISUALIZE shot you want to execute. Consider LIE of ball, DISTANCE desired, WIND, TERRAIN, OBSTACLES, intended ARC OF FLIGHT, and where you will lie for the NEXT shot. Select RIGHT club.

Take stance with feet in proper position in relation to DIRECTION line, POSITION of ball, TYPE of stance desired. DON'T reach out.

Position clubhead BEHIND ball with sole FLAT on ground and bottom edge of club SQUARE to direction line.

Place RIGHT hand on club with V pointing to RIGHT eye.

BALANCE weight, FLEX knees, WAGGLE clubhead to relieve TENSION.

Concentrate on SMOOTH, ONE-PIECE takeaway to start swing. Keep clubface SQUARE. DON'T rush.

PIVOT. Turn shoulders more than hips. Head STEADY. Break wrists NATURALLY to complete arc. PAUSE at top.

Start downswing with pull of LEFT arm, TURN of hips, return of LEFT heel to ground. RIGHT elbow brushes hip.

Delay uncocking WRISTS, until swing reaches HITTING ZONE, hands AHEAD of clubhead, THEN hit.

Concentrate on hitting THROUGH the ball toward hole.

Complete swing with FULL follow through, hands HIGH, weight on LEFT side, body facing HOLE.

HOW TO CHECK YOUR FAULTS

Most golfers wonder when they consistently play a particular shot poorly: "Why do I do that so often?"

To check major faults yourself, try to observe what may be causing the problem. Then go to the practice tee to try to find the remedy. The most common are:

● **Do you pull or push too many tee shots?**

You may not have enough left-hand and left-side control and may be gripping too loosely. Try gripping more firmly with last three fingers of left hand and let left side and firm left arm lead the clubhead. Or you may be swaying and coming through too soon or too late. Don't sway.

● **Do you often hit behind the ball—"fat" shots?**

This is usually caused by hitting from the top, so-called casting, or breaking wrists too soon on downswing. Try delaying your wrist break.

● **Do you skull—or blade—too many shots?**

You may be lifting hands abruptly on backswing. Start back left arm firm. Trust club's loft to lift ball.

● **Do you usually miss putts to left of the hole?**

You may be raising your head or breaking your wrists shortly before impact, causing you to pull (assuming that your putter face is properly aligned square to the line at address). Try to let your left hand dominate the stroke. Start club back with left hand and let it lead the clubhead through the ball. Minimize any wrist break.

● **Do your long putts usually die far short of hole?**

You probably make poor contact in trying to hit the ball hard. Concentrate on making solid contact. Extend backswing and follow through — rather than trying to strike the ball harder — to get the distance you need. You'll also get better direction.

PLAYING POINTERS

HOW TO EXERCISE PROPERLY

Proper exercises that strengthen the muscles most essential to better golf can be as helpful in improving your game as they are for experts like Gary Player, a fitness devotee.

To strengthen hands, wrists, forearms and legs, run in place or skip rope five minutes a day. Hold a pair of five or 10-pound weights and rotate your wrists a few minutes.

To stretch and strengthen all golf muscles, swing a weighted club or five-foot length of pipe. A 22-ounce training driver for men and a 16-ounce version for women, designed by Gene Sarazen, can be purchased.

Concentrate on building up your left hand. This can be done without much trouble almost anytime, such as at your desk or while reading or watching TV. You can squeeze a spring grip or a small rubber ball.

Another exercise is to swing a club back and forth using only your left hand. Pivot as usual and put your right knee into the swing. This will help minimize the fault of collapsing the left arm and quitting on a shot. It will also help you keep your left arm straight and develop a proper cocking of the wrist.

Isometric exercises have proved helpful in strengthening golf muscles and increasing distance.

Spread fingers far apart and press down on table with maximum strength for 15 seconds. Repeat 10 times.

Arm extended, hold golf club for five seconds with thumb, crook of forefinger and butt of hand.

Hold wedge extended in one hand, keeping elbow close against your side. Roll wrist so palm faces floor, then ceiling, holding each position six seconds.

Take your regular stance with a club. Hold club head against a door jamb at point you would normally hit a ball. Push hard. Hold for 10 seconds. Repeat.

Note: You might play better if you walk instead of ride.

HOW TO WARM UP

You can get off to a better start if you warm up before teeing off. Golfers limber up in various ways. These don't take too much time or trouble and will help:

On the way to your club, squeeze and release steering wheel to firm up grip, stressing pressure points.

Loosen your back and shoulder muscles by holding a club behind your back in the crook of your elbows and turning your body back and forth from the hips up. With legs spread wide, bend from hips with arms dangling. Swing arms left and right, touching opposite toes with fingertips.

Loosen fingers by holding a club horizontally in front of you and spinning it around with both hands.

Swing a wedge or 9-iron lazily but smoothly back and forth, starting with a half swing and gradually lengthening it, to loosen your wrists, get your rhythm and the feel of the club.

Don't rush the back-and-forth swing. Swing lazily, with lots of wrist action, letting the clubhead lag behind the hands and body turn as you would a weight on the end of a rope. Try a few swings with your left hand only.

Hit a few balls to give you the feel of making contact. Hit some chips and short wedge shots. Plastic, cotton or soft rubber practice balls will enable you to make contact with a full swing in a small area.

At the practice green, chip and putt to perfect your rhythm, judge distance and "get the feel." On putts, concentrate more on stroking the ball and judging the speed of the green.

If you can get on the practice tee, hit a half dozen balls with several irons and a couple of woods, working up from the wedge. Finish up with the driver or whatever other club you will be using on the first tee.

HOW TO PRACTICE EFFECTIVELY

Try to practice for a purpose, to correct some fault, improve some part of your game, or groove your swing. Don't, as so many do at driving ranges, just sock balls willy-nilly.

Proper practice can help you form good habits in checking details of your swing in search of faults.

Basically, you practice to repeat the correct grip, stance and swing so that through muscle memory they will become automatic. But first you must know what is correct. Otherwise you may be practicing your faults.

This usually requires the help of a professional, unless you're an expert yourself. Once you have detected and corrected your mistakes, practice the clubs with which you made them. Some pros say it helps to practice with your pet club in the category of the erring club. For example, if you're having trouble hitting the 2-wood, practice with a wood you like better, maybe the 3-wood. What you learn from hitting the 3-wood will be useful in hitting the 2-wood.

Practice all the kinds of shots you have to play during a round. That's the only way to learn to hit them well. This includes trouble shots from bad lies, hardpan, divot holes, rough, balls buried in sand and hillside lies. Practice especially short chip and pitch shots around the green and from bunkers.

Constant repetition is necessary to groove a swing for a particular shot. When he was coming up, Jack Nicklaus hit from 500 to 1,000 practice balls a day. Gary Player's skill with the sand wedge didn't come easily either. When he practiced greenside bunker shots years ago, he didn't quit until he had holed at least five.

CHECK POINTS: Grip, stance, balance, footwork and swing. To improve balance, hold finish on the follow through until ball has landed and stopped bouncing. Quarter, half and three-quarter swings help develop balance and feel. Use backswing practice to check control.

HOW TO HIT LONGER DRIVES

The long tee shot is one of golf's biggest thrills. It also helps lower your score by putting you in better position to birdie the par-5 and short par-4 holes and avoid bogeys — or worse.

Long hitters have special techniques they apply when they want to generate more power and get more distance off the tee or with fairway woods. Some of them you can try:

Grip the club in a "strong" position with left thumb on right side of shaft at about 2 o'clock. Hold tight throughout swing with last three fingers of left hand.

Take a slightly closed stance (right foot back from line of flight) with feet slightly wider apart.

Address ball more forward than usual, with left arm fully extended. Keep head behind ball.

Swing in as wide an arc as possible. Start clubhead straight back, low, with left hand in control. Don't break wrists until after hands pass right hip.

Make a full shoulder turn. Move left shoulder under chin. Keep left arm straight, head steady. Coil body muscles, which generate more power than arms and hands.

On downswing, dig in and push with right foot at impact. Hit through the ball, not at it, with both hands, with hands leading clubhead. Uncock wrists as late as possible in "crack-the-whip" fashion. Let clubhead follow flight of ball. Finish with arms high. You will get more roll if you strike ball at start of upswing. Also a hooked ball will roll farther.

UNUSUAL POINTERS: Slant tee forward when teeing ball. Strike ball on lettering; this avoids contact on hidden seams, gives more compression. Exhale on downswing. On cold days, drive with a warm ball from your pocket. If you are physically strong, use a high-compression ball.

HOW TO PUTT BETTER

STUDY. Examine putt from all sides. Notice roll of green and condition and grain of turf. Observe other player's putts. Calculate distance and determine force and direction of shot.

GRIP. Use grip most comfortable and successful for you. Reverse overlap most common. Back of left hand facing hole.

STANCE. Eyes directly over ball. Arms close to body. Clubface square to line. Weight favoring left side.

AIM. On long putts, concentrate more on distance than line. On curling putts allow for more break near hole. Let length of putt determine length of backswing. Visualize ball rolling into hole.

STROKE. Execute smooth stroke. Head and body steady. Strike ball sharply with sweet spot of blade, accelerating stroke into ball. Minimize wrists. Keep blade low and square.

CONFIDENCE. Think of striking ball solidly, and distance it must go. Shut out thoughts of missing.

PUTTING POINTERS

Learn to READ greens. Study CONTOUR, SPEED, TEX-TURE, CONDITION and GRAIN. Extra time taken to weigh effects these have on putts will pay off in strokes saved.

To find your putter's SWEET SPOT, let it hang free. Tap face until you find spot where tap doesn't turn it.

Ways to sharpen your putting skill:

Putt to target SMALLER than hole, such as ball, leaf or tee. This improves ACCURACY, makes real cup SEEM larger, improves CONFIDENCE when putting for KEEPS.

Practice LONG putts to improve stroke and timing.

Practice SHORT "payoff" putts. Drop several balls two feet from hole. See how many you can hole out in succession. Move back a foot every time you hole all balls.

PUTTING GAMES

Drop six balls a foot apart on each of three lines extending from hole. Start with closest and proceed in widening circles until you hole all 18. Lowest score wins.

Putt like playing horseshoes, using two balls. Score one point for each ball you put closest to hole, three for a hole-in-one, and six if you top it. 21 points wins.

PLUMB-BOB SYSTEM FOR DETERMINING LINE

First, find which eye is stronger. Sight object through hole in sheet of paper. Close each eye alternately. Eye with which you can still see object is stronger.

Stand 3-6 feet behind ball, facing hole. Hold putter near BOT-TOM of grip with thumb and forefinger and at arm's length. With BOTH eyes sight lower part of shaft on ball and line up with hole. Close WEAKER eye. If holes stays in line with shaft, putting line is STRAIGHT. If hole falls to one side, ball will break to SAME side.

HOW TO READ THE GREENS

Good putting involves more than striking the ball properly. Being able to judge how it will roll can be equally vital. So it pays to "read the greens."

First note how the green slopes when you play your approach. As you walk up to the green, take note of its contours relative to your ball and the hole.

Your first steps on the green can give you a feel of whether it is hard — and fast — or plush and soft, thus slow. That's also the time to check the grass. The ball will travel faster on fine and closely cut turf, when grain is with you, and downhill. A cross grain will curve the ball in direction the grass blades lie.

Grass will look shiny when grain is with you, dark when it's against you. Approach your ball on a line with the hole so you can judge the contour from a distance. Note whether your line deviates from the general slope. While awaiting your turn, notice how other putts roll.

Crouch a few feet behind your ball to sight hole and line. Consider slope, grain and speed. If in doubt, sight from opposite side, from cup to ball. Some good putters like to sight from low side, uphill. Side view helps judge distance.

If green is wet, or slow otherwise, your putt will not break as much as you might expect.

Study area around hole most carefully; it has most effect on a slowing ball. On sidehill putt, note where ball can best enter cup. Uneven depth of dirt above rim of metal cup can reveal a slope in green.

TIPS TO REMEMBER:

First impressions are usually correct.

Ball will "break" less when green is slow or wet. When grass looks shiny, you are looking with the grain; when dark, you are looking against it.

Putt more firmly over spike marks and footprints.

HOW TO JUDGE CLUB DISTANCES

How far should you hit a golf ball with each club?

Average distances for average players under normal conditions are listed below. But few players get the same distance.

What's important to you is what YOU can expect from each club. To help you improve your game, fill in the last column with the average distance YOU can count on with each club, and refer to it when playing until you know it.

CLUB	OLD NAME	LOFT IN DEGREES	AVERAGE DISTANCE Men	Women	YOUR DISTANCE
1 Wood	Driver	11	220	190	280-300
2 Wood	Brassie	14	210	180	—
3 Wood	Spoon	17	200	170	250-260
4 Wood	Cleek	20	190	160	220-250
5 Wood	Baffy	23	180	150	200-220
1 Iron	Driving Iron	19	190	160	—
2 Iron	Mid-Iron	23	180	150	—
3 Iron	Mid-Mashie	27	170	140	—
4 Iron	Mashie Iron	31	160	130	180-200
5 Iron	Mashie	35	150	120	—
6 Iron	Spade Mashie	39	140	110	—
7 Iron	Mashie Niblick	43	130	100	160-180
8 Iron	Pitcher	47	120	90	150-160
9 Iron	Niblick	51	110	80	140-150
Pitching Wedge		55	90	65	120-140
Sand Wedge		59	70	50	-120

TIP: In shooting to a green, remember what club you need from 150-yard marker. Then, for every 10 yards you are CLOSER to hole, take one less club (one number higher); for every 10 yards you are FARTHER from hole, take one more club (one number lower). Take into account pin position.

POINTERS FOR BEGINNERS

Many golfers start the easy way as caddies or junior golfers. This page is primarily for those who are taking up golf without such previous experience.

Most important is to get started right. See a golf professional first. A wrong start can instill bad habits which will make it harder for you to improve your game later.

It's not necessary to buy an expensive set of clubs or any clubs at all, at the outset. You shouldn't invest in clubs until you are sure you are going to stick with the game and have some idea what make of clubs you will like. The pro usually has clubs he'll let you use for awhile.

Even when you're ready to buy clubs you may want to start with a good used set. Most pro shops have them.

Once in the hands of a professional, follow his advice. It will take at least six half-hour lessons and many weeks to learn the game, the exact number depending on the skill you want to achieve and your rate of progress.

Some professionals start with group lessons at reduced cost. These might be desirable if private lessons make you self-concious or you can't afford them.

Your pro will tell you how, what, and how much to practice and when you can start playing. Consider taking a playing lesson. Ask your pro what ball to use.

It will also help you to get a good start if you are familiar with The Rules of Golf, golf etiquette and golf terms. The most important and useful are in this Guide.

Read and observe as much as you can about golf. Illustrated golf magazines and books and watching golf pros on TV, will help you develop your game.

A final point: Do your learning on the practice tee, not while playing. Says Lionel Callaway, famous pro: "Learn to play; don't play to learn."

POINTERS FOR WOMEN

USE A LOW-COMPRESSION BALL. Keep grip firm throughout swing. Women's tendency to loosen at top causes loss of control. Keep last three fingers of left hand snug, left thumb in groove of right hand and welded against it.

GRIP FOR DISTANCE. Take "strong" grip, turning hands to right so that V formed by left thumb and index finger points to right shoulder instead of chin.

FOR SMALL HANDS, try the unlap (10-finger) or interlocking grip. Jack Nicklaus uses the interlocking grip, says it keeps his hands working more in unison.

DON'T OVERSWING. Extreme body turn, with club dropping below level at top, causes sway, upsets timing. Shorter swing will give better control, make solid contact with ball easier, and give more distance with less effort.

POWER SWING. Delay uncocking of wrists until hands approach hitting zone. Get hips out of way. Then lash clubhead in one explosive action.

USE WOODS MORE, particularly 4, 5 and 6-wood. Larger club-face helps you get ball airborne more easily. Very helpful when wind's at your back. Woods don't require as strenuous a swing as irons with same loft. Address ball in center of stance. Use sweeping stroke, not down-and-through.

IN CHIPPING, swing from shoulders and, at last instant, hit crisply with hands. Accent weight on left foot and keep it there. Don't shift. Keep hands well ahead of ball. (Hands behind ball causes scuffing.) Keep feet close together.

IN PUTTING, wide stance makes firm foundation, helps avoid sway. Less wrist break reduces chances of error.

37

POINTERS FOR SENIORS

As you get older you can actually **improve** your golf game, as well as keep it from slipping, if you work on it in the right way.

In your senior years—past 50—you begin to lose zip and strength, but your golf game need not suffer. There are ways you can compensate for this physical change which could even lower your score if practiced enough.

CLUBS. Use lighter clubs with longer and whippier shafts to give you a bigger arc and more clubhead speed. The driver can be two inches longer than normal for you; the other woods proportionately less longer. Use woods more than long irons. The 5 wood is commonly used and even deeper faced woods are gaining popularity.

SWING. Let your wrists work more. Relax them and strive for a full break at the top of your backswing. Take a fuller pivot and longer swing—slow, relaxed, with accent on rhythm rather than power—and whip the clubhead through the ball with a full follow-through. Feel and swing clubhead.

GRIP. A strong grip is essential for power, but older golfers tend to turn the right hand too far under the shaft, causing smothered hooks. You can get a strong enough grip if you point the V formed by the thumb and forefinger of your left hand toward your right shoulder, and the V of your right hand toward your right eye. You should feel some tension in your forearms at address.

SPECIAL TIPS: If overweight, turn right foot out more to help you get fuller pivot. For more loft take higher backswing. For more control and power with irons, address ball forward with 3-iron, in middle with others. Don't use 2-wood except on tee. Leave 2-iron home. To make up for lack of distance, concentrate on your short game around the green and on your putting. Use a low-compression ball.

HOW YOUR PRO CAN HELP YOU

The club pro is a golfer's best friend, for he is dedicated to helping you play better and solve your golfing problems.

Besides giving you regular lessons, he's available to give you playing lessons. This alone can knock several strokes off your score. (See Playing Lessons.)

Your pro will fit you with the right clubs that are best for your game, store them, clean them and make minor repairs.

He will help you learn the rules and settle arguments.

Your pro is the club's public relations man. He will send news of your golf achievements to the papers, or help you get rewards when you score a hole-in-one.

He's always available to look over your swing when you're having a small problem and give helpful advice about anything that may be troubling your game.

If your pro competes in local PGA pro-amateur events, he probably takes several club members along to be his partners. Ask to be included. The competition will help you.

Golf balls are made to resist varying amounts of compression, with a variety of covers, to suit all kinds of players. The 100 compression ball with a very thin cover is best for pros and low-handicap players (especially in hot weather). A 90 ball is best for long hitters and better-than-average golfers. Senior golfers and particularly women are better off and will likely get more distance with a softer, 60-80 compression ball. Your pro can advise you as to what compression ball is best for you if he is familiar with your game.

Whether you patronize your pro or not, you are benefiting from his many services, without which the club could not function satisfactorily. If he is a typical pro, he depends on your patronage to make his living.

When you do not patronize him, you are shifting to other club members your share of the responsibility.

HOW TO TAKE LESSONS

If you are a beginner, don't try to learn the game by yourself. See a professional and sign up for some lessons.

Tell him what previous sports experience you've had. It will make it easier for him to help you because he will know what muscles and coordination you have developed.

He can suggest exercises to build up the muscles you will use most in playing golf.

If you are an experienced golfer, tell your pro what your problem is — that you are slicing, hooking or topping the ball, or not getting the distance you should.

Listen to what he tells you, and follow instructions. Don't try to tell HIM what you are doing wrong. When he checks your swing he'll know.

Try to understand what your pro tells you. When he says to make this correction or that, try to understand why. If you don't know, ask him to explain it again.

Don't be disturbed if the correction, such as in your grip or swing, doesn't "feel right." It usually doesn't until you become accustomed to it.

Be realistic about your physical limitations and potential capabilities, and set your standard of achievement accordingly. Don't try to be something you can't.

Don't expect to learn everything in one lesson. Go back to your pro and the practice tee frequently.

Try to make notes and stick to what your pro has told you to do. Don't give up easily and return to old errors because they come naturally and may feel comfortable.

Above all, practice what you learn, and practice frequently to retain it. Practice on the practice tee or green, not on the course. The best time is right after a lesson. Some golfers like to practice right after a round to correct mistakes and polish the rough spots out of their game.

HOW PLAYING LESSONS HELP

A playing lesson serves an entirely different purpose from one on the practice tee. Beginners find it especially useful.

On the practice tee you are taught how to hit the ball and use each club. From a playing lesson you learn how the game is played under actual conditions.

You are taught aspects of golf which are difficult to grasp except under playing conditions.

Etiquette is one. This is a much neglected part of the beginner's education. On the course, your pro can tell you where to stand when others are playing a shot; how to walk in and out of bunkers, smooth footprints; where to walk and how to act on the putting green; how to mark your ball.

In a playing lesson you should learn:

How to study a hole from the tee and visualize how to play it so as to avoid hazards and other risks.

How to recognize and play a strategic hole, such as a dogleg, which calls for playing to a position which will enable you to make a successful next shot.

When to gamble because the odds are in your favor and the risk from failure minimal.

How to judge distances, select clubs and improve your judgment of distance you get from each.

When and how to play low, high, punch, chip, pitch or other types of shots to the green. How to play trouble shots.

How to judge the contours of greens and the effect they will have on approach shots and putts.

Perhaps as important as all of these is just watching your pro play — observing and absorbing some of his style and technique, and how he thinks.

Imitation is a great aid in learning how to play better golf, and you'll find no better opportunity than to imitate your pro right on the spot.

HOW TO FIND TIME AND KEEP FIT

The average golfer has trouble finding time to play golf and keep fit between infrequent rounds. Some tips:

Make time to play by going out before or after work. One golfer plays six holes before breakfast, uses three balls, feels he's played "compact 18."

After work, try to get in nine holes or hit practice balls a few times a week. At least practice chipping and putting.

Entertain clients or prospects at golf instead of lunch.

Arrange to play on a business trip when you'll wind up by noon. Your club membership card will be honored by most clubs if you have no friend to introduce you.

Plan business meetings at one of the growing number of golf resorts which welcome them.

With longer vacations, you might use some of your vacation time for long week-end golf trips.

Do house and yard chores during the week, when possible, to leave you free for golf on weekends.

Develop a family interest in golf. It will make it easier for you to get out, either because you'll be playing with the family or they'll be playing more golf than you — and won't begrudge your playing.

On weekends, play early in morning or afternoon, so that you will have half a day at home or with the family. Teeing off at 10 or 11 tends to kill the whole day.

TIPS FOR KEEPING FIT BETWEEN ROUNDS:

Swing a 22-ounce club every evening. Keep and use a spring grip in your desk at the office. Carry and squeeze a small rubber ball. Practice chip shots in your yard, putting in your living room. Finger-tip push-ups help strengthen hands. Patronize practice ranges. Walking briskly will strengthen your legs and improve your wind.

42

GOLF STRATEGY

PLAYING STRATEGY

You can improve your scoring by using your head and playing **every** shot as if it were the most important. You've probably noticed many times how a single miscue ruined a good score or cost you a match. In many ways golf is a game of avoiding mistakes.

ON THE DRIVE — Look first for any trouble ahead you want to avoid. Then look for the best position to place your tee shot in relation to possible trouble and best approach to the green. Consider the terrain and the best way to take advantage of slopes and avoid hazards.

ON PAR 3'S — Play to the safer side of green. If the shot requires a long iron or wood, consider playing short or to some other safe area, then pitching or chipping to the hole for a possible par or easy bogey.

ON THE FAIRWAY — Again, study the shot from all angles. Should you go for the green or play safe? Where's the trouble? Any hazards to carry? Will the ball kick to left or right? Will the green hold the shot? Is it uphill or into the wind and requires a longer club than usual for the distance? Is your lie tight, downhill, sidehill?

ON SHORT APPROACH SHOTS — Always plan to have the ball land on the green if possible. Bounce and roll will be more reliable. On longer approaches, pitch to the pin if the greens are holding. On shorter shots, try to use as much green as possible. Chip to the edge with a club whose loft will give your ball the proper arc to permit it to run the distance to the cup. (See Chipping.)

FROM SAND NEAR GREEN — Don't reach automatically for your wedge. From a shallow trap, you might do better by chipping or, if the lip is smooth and your lie good, using your putter — the "Texas wedge."

THINK YOUR WAY TO BETTER SCORING

Many mistakes that raise your score are caused by not thinking of **all** the factors before you make a shot, or by thinking incorrectly. Having no relationship to skill, they can be avoided by any golfer. You can think your way to better golf through better decision-making and better management.

DECISION-MAKING — Be decisive. Decide quickly what club you will use and convince yourself it is the right one. When lining up a putt, decide how it will break and how hard to hit it, then hit it before you can change your mind.

In reaching a decision, consider your limitations, particularly when you're in trouble. Go with the percentages. Don't think you can make a miracle shot to make up for a bad one. And don't gamble unless the stakes and your chances make it worthwhile.

GAME MANAGEMENT — Prepare psychologically to play each hole to the best of your ability. Proper self-examination can help you recognize a defective pattern in your game.

Consider whether you play poorer at the beginning, middle or end of a round, and try to analyze why.

Do you get careless, ease up, and take unnecessary chances when ahead, or tense up and become erratic when behind? Do you gamble at the wrong time?

Try to keep an even temperament. Don't lose your poise. Take everything in stride, failures as well as successes.

This way you can concentrate on what you have to do at the moment — not on what just happened or what may come up at the next hole. Play each stroke and each hole as if it were the only stroke and only hole you are going to play that day. This kind of thinking is bound to pay off in lower scores.

HOW TO CONCENTRATE

You must concentrate to score well and win. Golfers with ability to concentrate on their own games can win over others with greater skill but poor mental attitude.

Losers are disturbed by minor distractions or let their mind wander, like the young pro who blew a five-shot lead and lost a chance to win his first pro tournament because he kept thinking of the various rewards victory would bring him — instead of concentrating on his game.

To help you concentrate, groove your mental attitude toward a good swing. Ignore your opponent for the most part. Play your own game, not his. Stay loose by concentrating on what **you** are doing; let your opponent do the watching and worrying. So says one of the loosest players of all time, Julius Boros.

Stand closer to ball. This will relax motion of legs and feet and put more feel and control in hands. Slow your game a little so you won't hurry your shots.

After you've taken your stance, however, don't slow down to the point that tension builds up and you waver and begin to wonder how you're going to hit the shot.

Try to do as much as you can naturally, from muscle memory, without conscious effort.

Try not to think of too many things, but think positively, think of good shots you made before with same club and feel that all your shots will be good ones.

Stick to fundamentals. Don't experiment while playing. Play the shots you know you can play well and use the clubs you know you can hit.

Maintain your confidence at all times. Confidence and clear thinking rank high among touring pros who know that mental attitude often is more important than technical skill in winning tournaments.

HOW TO WIN MATCHES

Strategy in winning golf matches begins with being prepared. Avoid pre-match tension. Warm up.

Try to follow normal routine before your match. Set aside problems. Eat several hours before tee off time. Feel confident you can win. Never go into a match thinking your chances of winning are less than 50-50.

The earlier you tee off, the longer warm-up you'll need.

Try your best on early holes. Remember, on the card the first hole counts as much as the last. Actually, it counts more, because winning the early holes will give **you** a psychological advantage. Your opponent may start pressing hard to catch you and make mistakes.

Never take your opponent lightly or be overly generous when ahead. Beat him the best you can.

When Al Watrous was 9 up with 12 holes to play in a 36-hole PGA championship match in 1932, he conceded Bobby Cruickshank a five-foot putt for a half. This so inspired Bobby that he won on the fifth extra hole, proving another point: Never give up until the final putt.

Retain a positive attitude, but avoid overconfidence. Play safe when you're ahead and gamble when you're behind, but don't take risks when you don't need to.

Don't compound your mistakes by following one mistake with another. It's easier to save strokes than gain them.

Learn from your opponent. When possible note the club he uses when you face a similar shot. Watch the roll and speed of his ball on the green.

Finally, retain the will to win. Don't ease up when ahead; don't give up when behind.

Knowing the strategy of match play can help you beat a better player. (See How to Win Four-Ball Matches.)

HOW TO WIN FOUR-BALL MATCHES

Four-ball, or so-called best-ball matches offer many opportunities to utilize strategy to win.

To begin with, much depends at the outset on how you pair up. If you have a choice, select a steady player if you are wild and inclined to run into some bad holes. If steady and can pretty much hold your own, get a partner who might shoot some spectacular holes and win them.

Unless one has a preference, let the straighter driver hit first. Once he's put his tee shot in good position, then the other can let out shaft or try to cut a dog-leg. Likewise, if one can get safely on the green for a par, the other can go for the pin for a birdie.

Try to keep both balls in play at all times so as not to pressure one partner with a two-on-one situation.

On the green, when both partners have makeable putts, the one with easier putt should try first. He's more likely to make it if he knows his partner still has a crack at it. The hole shrinks if your partner misses before you putt.

Let your partner hole out first if he has a makeable putt to halve and you have a long one to win. Then you can go for it and not worry about losing if you three-putt.

Avoid putting if you can when you are away and your putt is on the same line as a closer opponent and will help him judge roll or speed. Let your partner hole out if his score will be as good as you could do, then pick up. This is also advisable if your partner can get down ahead of an opponent. This puts pressure on your opponent instead of his putting pressure on your partner.

Concede an opponent's putt, if he's away and not in contention if his putt would help his partner with the line. His side loses the hole if he insists on putting.

HOW TO PLAY UNDER PRESSURE

If you can cope with pressure, you will win more "big ones" than expected, and score more upsets. Ability to handle tense situations separates the men from the boys at your club as well as on the pro Tour. Good competitors have perfected ways to deal with tension which help them. Here are some:

Be natural. Develop a pattern of pre-shot movements and don't vary them under pressure. Keep an even pace. Develop a set routine and stick with it on every shot.

Think positively. Visualize how a good shot will look and feel. Don't worry about missing a putt or going into a bunker or pond, or more than likely you will.

Concentrate so hard you shut out distractions. When addressing the ball, concentrate on hitting it well, not on the result you hope for. Don't think of the consequences of erring.

Try to minimize the importance of the stroke or competition. Don't think of the trophy you will get if you win.

Don't lose your temper. When you flub a shot, just concentrate on the next one. Have faith that you can scramble and get the stroke back.

Try to play under pressure often to get accustomed to it. Get in the habit of playing ALL shots as if they were important, then when you face a really important one that might decide a match, it shouldn't make much, if any, difference.

Taking deep breaths helps relax you. When about to putt, exhale, then hold it while you stroke the ball.

Stay in motion, waggling club and wiggling feet, when addressing the ball. Don't freeze over it.

TIPS TO FIGHT TENSION: Slow your backswing . . . when scared, hit hard . . . choke down on your grip . . . stick to fundamentals . . . think out every shot . . . study conditions carefully . . . never let yourself be rushed . . . believe in yourself . . . act naturally, stick to normal routines.

HOW TO SCRAMBLE AND WIN

Your short game deserves special attention because it's played in the scoring zone where physical strength does not count. You can beat an otherwise better player if you get the ball in the hole from any situation without wasting strokes. This calls for good scrambling.

Scrambling is the art of saving strokes. Every golfer gets into some trouble, even the best of them. But a good scrambler will minimize the damage by good recoveries that save a par or bogey — and stun the opposition.

Average golfers have to scramble more than good ones, so should practice more with the scoring clubs — short iron and putter. Getting close to the hole with short irons, and putting reasonably well, will make you a better-than-average scorer. For a short hitter, good scrambling can be his survival kit against the longer hitters.

Develop skill with all short irons. Select the right club to fit the circumstances and let it do the work. The close-in pitch shot is often a good scrambler's secret weapon, so practice it with your favorite club.

Reading greens accurately is most helpful in getting approach up for needed one-putt. Check contour and speed. On putts concentrate more on distance than line.

On chips, land ball on green and run it up if pin is far enough back, rather than lob it to pin. Aim at spot on green where you want ball to land. Use straight-face club uphill, more lofted club downhill.

Chipping with 5 or 6-iron, aim 1/3 of distance, figure ball will roll other 2/3. With 7 or 8-iron, carry ball halfway. With 9-iron or wedge, pitch 2/3 of distance.

GENERAL TIPS — Don't let trouble upset you. Keep your composure. Be decisive. Concentrate. Picture result you expect. Play all trouble shots with complete confidence.

HOW TO PLAY OUT OF TROUBLE

How many times have you lost a hole you thought you had "in the bag" because your opponent was in trouble? These tips will help **you** pull the surprises:

USE YOUR HEAD — This is one of the first rules. You may not be in as much trouble as you think. Study your situation, the specific problem, and how best to solve it. Should you play safe or gamble? If you gamble, be sure it's worth the risk. In either case, look out for other trouble you might get into.

PLAN YOUR RECOVERY — Getting out of trouble requires both sound planning and execution. Visualize how you want the ball to travel and where you want it to stop. Decide what club to use, how to play the shot, then think only of hitting the ball well. Don't worry about the outcome, or be over-anxious. Anxiety has spoiled many a good recovery attempt.

OUT OF THE WOODS — Two avenues of recovery from trees are through an opening or under the branches. Before you try going through an opening, consider the odds, what you'll gain, and what it might cost if you fail. The best rule is to play it safe unless you're behind and need to gamble.

WHEN STYMIED — If there's a tree or other obstacle in your way, stand behind the ball to judge how much clearance you have. You'll get a more accurate view of your line from behind than from where you address the ball. If you're stymied, concentrate not on the obstacle but aim at an object in the distance that is as close as possible to the direction you want the ball to go and still get you safely by the obstacle.

IN DEEP BUNKER — Close to a steep bank, consider playing out safely to either side or even back toward the tee. If you do try to clear the steep bank, be sure to swing extra hard with a big backswing and high follow-through.

BURIED BALL IN SAND — Choke down on grip, close clubface, open stance more, play ball back. Swing upright, break wrists. Hit farther behind ball than normal trap shot. Strike hard and deep. Follow through. Consider using 9-iron instead of wedge.

OUT OF ROUGH — Take a more lofted club to get ball up quickly. Take one less (higher number) club than usual for distance desired to allow for extra roll. Strike down, abruptly, with more wrists. Don't sweep.

SHORT PITCH FROM THICK ROUGH — Use wedge. Play ball back of center. Swing more upright, slowly, gently. Hit down and make full follow through.

OFF BARE GROUND — When ball lies on bare ground, keep hands ahead of clubhead, contact ball before ground.

BALL IN DIVOT HOLE — Keep hands ahead of ball, most of weight on left side. Strike descending blow.

CUT SHOT — Using wedge or 9-iron, play ball off left heel with narrow, open stance. Grip club with left hand turned slightly to left to allow clubface to open at impact. Execute leisurely upright swing with firm wrists, allowing clubhead to slice under ball.

LEFT-HANDED SHOT — Use a high-numbered iron with more clubface. Reverse grip, left hand below right. Invert club so that toe or tip of clubhead becomes sole. Turn clubface to give desired loft. Swing left-handed. It takes lots of practice to pull this shot off well.

FENCE SHOT — When ball lies near fence that is on opposite side of where you must stand, close clubface inward. Ball will fly toward safe ground. When fence is where you would stand, try left-handed shot or even a backward shot between your legs.

HOW TO PLAY THE PAR 3'S

It pays to plan carefully for playing par 3 holes. Most courses have four of them. Threes on these holes can do a lot for your score and give you a psychological lift. So make the most of the opportunity.

In selecting your club, forget your ego. Take as much club as you will need to carry ball to the pin. A check at one event showed 90 percent of tee shots stopping short of hole; 40 percent short of green. So consider taking a longer club than you might expect to use.

Consider distance to the pin, not green. It can vary one or two clubs, depending on pin placement and position of tee markers. Remember: Distance on card is from middle of tee to middle of green.

Consider also the wind. Tossing some grass on the tee is not enough. The wind may be blowing differently at the green, where its effect is greatest. So check the flag and tops of trees near the green.

Another distance factor is green elevation. If it's elevated, better add 10 yards; lower, deduct 10.

Knowing you have correct club will increase confidence, help you make a smooth swing. You don't want to force the swing. That would affect your rhythm and swing arc. This should be a control shot.

Always use a tee, but keep the ball close to turf so you can take divot and get backspin with iron. Value of a tee was expressed by Gene Sarazen. Asked why he used a tee when many top amateurs simply place the ball on turf, he replied: "I play for money."

TIP TO REMEMBER — Swing well within yourself.

HOW TO PLAY IN WET WEATHER

You can give yourself an advantage when playing under wet conditions by following these suggestions:

BE PREPARED — When rain threatens, carry rain gear — umbrella, hat, jacket, rubbers or rubber shoes, rain pants for heavy rain, large towel and extra gloves.

PROTECT YOURSELF AND EQUIPMENT — Keep umbrella and towel over self and clubs as much as possible. Dry clubheads and grips after each shot. In lightning storm, you may stop play. (See The Rules of Golf.)

ADJUST YOUR GAME TO CONDITIONS — Remember that the turf will be softer, the grass more clinging, the sand wetter and heavier, and that your ball won't roll as far in the wet grass.

Make sure your feet are firmly planted so you won't slip when you swing.

Address ball farther forward and sweep ball off grass with less divot than usual.

Shorten your swing to about three-quarters normal.

On chip shots, use deeper faced club for longer carry, such as 7-iron instead of 5-iron.

Hit putts harder, more off left toe for overspin, and allow for less "break" than usual.

KNOW RULES FOR CASUAL WATER — They're in your favor. You may lift without penalty if your ball is in, or touches, or you must stand in casual water.

On the green, you may move your ball, not closer to hole, to avoid casual water between your ball and hole.

In a bunker, you may lift out of water and drop in sand without penalty, not nearer hole. With one stroke penalty, you may drop the ball behind bunker.

HOW TO PLAY IN HEAT AND COLD

These are tips good players have found effective in hot or cold weather which will help your game:

HOT WEATHER TIPS — Conserve energy by walking slower, staying in shade. Reduce warm-up to minimum.

Wear loose and light-colored clothes. Also cap, hat or peak. Absorbent band is especially helpful in keeping perspiration off eyeglasses. Carry an umbrella if sun is hot.

Carry towels to wipe perspiration off hands, forearms, face and forehead, as well as grips of clubs.

If you wear a golf glove, carry one or two spares to change when one gets wet. Remove glove between shots.

Take coated salt tablets — two before teeing off and two more after nine holes. Eat lightly. Don't over-drink.

COLD WEATHER TIPS — For keeping warm, several layers of light clothing are more effective than one heavy garment. Consider long or thermal underwear or pajamas, rainpants, rubbers, nylon windbreaker, wool dickie, sweaters, stocking hat, two pairs of socks.

Rub and blow on hands, keep them in pockets, tucked under arms, carry handwarmer, loose mittens.

Loosen grip, swing slower and easier, but with fuller body turn. Take less divot.

Remember: Ground will be harder. Greens won't hold, will be slower and rougher. Hooked balls will go farther because they will stay low into wind and roll more.

Ball won't carry as far, so take more club than usual.

Use ball with lower compression. Keep balls in warm room overnight or place in lukewarm water before using. Carry extra ball in pocket or near handwarmer. Change ball, every hole. (Use of devices specifically designed to warm golf balls violates Rule 37-9a, Decision 69-36.)

TIPS FOR TOURNAMENT COMPETITION

Don't waste your hard-earned skill in a tournament by some foolish misstep or ignorance of how to conduct yourself. In any competition, there are certain rules and practices it is well to know and observe.

At all times, of course, be familiar with The Rules of Golf. Also know any local or special rules for the tournament. Read the rules on the score card. Ignorance of a rule can make the difference between winning and losing.

Carrying more than 14 clubs can cost you up to two holes in match play, four strokes in medal play for each excess club. You can also be penalized for slow play.

In playing a match, if any dispute or doubt arises on any point, any claim should be made before you tee off on the next hole. In medal play you may play an alternate ball.

Report to the tee with your caddie at least 10 minutes before tee off time. Locate your opponents and partner.

Mark several balls with your own identification before starting. Use a marking pen or a spot of nail polish. Playing wrong ball will cost you a penalty.

In match play, you have the honor on the first hole if you are higher on the pairings sheet. It is also your duty to keep score and turn in the card with the result.

On completion of a round in stroke play, check the card carefully before signing it and return it immediately to scorer. Correct score by holes is most important.

In a tournament away from your club, try to play the course before the tournament begins or at least "walk" the course, noting terrain, hazards, blind approaches and other features. Be sure your entry is properly prepared and received in time. Julius Boros won the USGA Open in 1963 but couldn't even try for it the year before because his entry was late.

RULES, GAMES
AND MATCHES

YOUR RIGHTS UNDER THE RULES

Too few golfers realize that the USGA's Rules of Golf protect as well as penalize them. You can save many strokes by knowing your rights on the golf course—the many things you **MAY** do—and utilizing them.

A case in point is Arnold Palmer's winning his first Masters in 1958 by one stroke, instead of finishing third. He simply insisted on his right, under a local rule, to a free lift when his ball became embedded in a mound. It saved him two strokes, just enough to win.

Ironically, by forgetting the provisional ball rule in effect at the time, Palmer was disqualified from the 1963 Bing Crosby and broke a string of 47 finishes in the money.

IN GENERAL

RECEIVING ADVICE—You may ask and take advice from your caddie, your partner or his caddie.

PLAYING OUT OF TURN—There is no penality. In match play, your opponent may have you replay the shot.

RELIEF FROM LOOSE IMPEDIMENTS—Except in hazard, you may move natural objects not fixed or growing.

RELIEF FROM OBSTRUCTION—You are entitled to relief without penalty from any artificial object or structure which interferes with your stance or swing. (Exceptions: Walls, fences or stakes which define out-of-bounds.) Included are pipes, rakes, buildings, artificial paths, hoses, benches and ball washers. If the obstruction is immovable, you may drop without penalty not more than one club length from the nearest spot not nearer the hole which provides relief. You may not measure through an obstruction, except a path or when the ball lies in or on the obstruction. When in a hazard, you must drop in the hazard.

YOUR RIGHTS UNDER THE RULES (Cont.)

PLAYING WRONG BALL—In match play, you win hole if your opponent plays a wrong ball, except in hazard. In four-ball, offender's partner is not penalized unless violation assisted partner. In stroke play, penalty is two strokes. Except in hazard, you may lift ball to identify it in presence of others.

UNPLAYABLE LIE—You are the sole judge of whether your ball is unplayable. With one stroke penalty you may drop within two club lengths to either side or back as far as you like. Or you may replay from the previous position with stroke-and-distance penalty.

DAMAGED BALL—On a hole in which your ball becomes so damaged as to be unfit for play, you may replace it without penalty after declaring your intention. Opponent or marker may dispute your claim and appeal to referee or committee.

PROVISIONAL BALL—You may play a provisional ball for one which may be out-of-bounds or lost outside of a water hazard (or in hazard if local rule permits) after announcing your intention. You may keep playing the ball as a provisional until you reach area of original ball.

CASUAL WATER & GROUND UNDER REPAIR—If your ball is in, or you have to stand in, casual water or ground under repair, you get a free drop within one club length from a point that provides complete relief from nearest margin of area, not nearer hole. If ball lies in bunker, you must drop within bunker. With one stroke penalty, you may drop outside. Consider snow and ice as casual water or loose impediments.

OPPONENT'S STROKES—In match play, you are entitled during play of a hole to ask your opponent how many strokes he's taken. You win the hole if he gives wrong information.

PRACTICE ON COURSE—There's no penalty for practicing on the course on the day you are to play a match.

14 CLUBS—Maximum penalty for carrying more than 14 clubs is two holes in match play, four strokes in stroke play.

YOUR RIGHTS UNDER THE RULES (Cont.)

ON THE TEE

ACCIDENTALLY KNOCKING BALL OFF TEE—No penalty.
TEEING OFF IN FRONT OF MARKERS—No penalty in match play. You must replay shot if opponent requests. In stroke play, two strokes penalty and you must then play from within the teeing ground.

IN A HAZARD

OBSTRUCTION—You're entitled to same relief in hazard as elsewhere, except that you must drop in hazard.
YOU MAY SMOOTH SAND IN BUNKER after you've played stroke it it doesn't improve lie of ball still in hazard or assist you in subsequent play of the hole.
YOU MAY LAY EXTRA CLUBS IN HAZARD before playing out if you don't improve lie or test soil.
PLAYING WRONG BALL. There's no penalty for playing wrong ball out of hazard if you then play your own.

ON THE GREEN

FLAGSTICK—There's no penalty for ball striking unattended flagstick if it was played from off the green. Any penalty for striking an attended pin is against the player, no matter who attended it. While playing a blind shot, you may have the flagstick held up to indicate the position of the hole.
LIFTING BALL—In a singles match, your opponent may lift his ball; however, he must replace it immediately if you request. Leaving it may sometimes help you, because there's no penalty if your ball strikes it. In a four-ball match, any player may have any ball marked. In stroke play, however, a player closer to the hole has the option to lift or putt out.
BALL STRIKING ANOTHER BALL—In match play, there's no penalty when your ball strikes another.

If your ball is struck and moved by another, you have the option in a singles match to leave it where it lies or replace it; in four-ball competition you must replace it.

PUTTING OUT OF TURN—In a four-ball match, either partner may putt when one is away. It's good strategy sometimes for closer partner to putt first.

BALL HANGING ON LIP—Opponent is allowed only "a few seconds" — not more than 10 — to decide whether ball may drop. After that you may concede next putt, knocking ball away.

CASUAL WATER—If casual water (or ground under repair) intervenes between ball on green and the hole, you may move your ball without penalty to nearest point which affords maximum relief, but not nearer hole.

CONCEDED PUTT—If opponent concedes your putt, he may not retract it should you happen to tap the ball anyhow and miss. In four-ball match one must accept the concession. If opponent insists on putting (to help partner see the break) partner is disqualified from hole.

REPAIRING BALL MARK OR HOLE PLUG—Any ball mark or old hole plug on the green may be repaired in any manner, including stepping on it, even if on the line of putt. This privilege does not extend to spike, shoe or other marks or blemishes.

CLEANING BALL—On putting green you may lift ball to clean it or for any purpose you wish. You may also clean ball when lifting from water hazard, obstruction, unplayable lie, casual water, ground under repair,embedded lie or a wrong green.

EMBEDDED BALL—Ball embedded in any closely mown area not in hazard may be lifted without penalty.

NOTE: The foregoing rules interpretations are unofficial. For official rules, consult The Rules of Golf or contact the USGA Headquarters, Far Hills, New Jersey 07931.

MATCH PLAY RULES TO REMEMBER

On putting green, player controls whether opponent's ball nearer hole may be lifted or left to assist him.

There's no penalty if your putt strikes opponent's ball. He has option, if ball is moved, to leave it (even if in cup) or replace it. In four-ball, he **must** replace.

You lose hole if your putt strikes flagstick.

There's no penalty for playing out of turn. Opponent may require you to replay stroke. Same applies if you tee off in front of markers. In four-ball, partners may play their shots out of turn when either is away.

If you play a wrong ball, you lose hole. If opponents play each other's ball, the first to err loses. If that can't be determined, hole shall be played out with exchanged balls.

If your ball strikes your opponent, his caddie or equipment, you may play ball as it lies or replay the stroke without penalty. If it strikes you, your partner, your caddies or your equipment, you lose hole.

If you give advice to, or ask advice from, your opponent or his caddie, you lose the hole.

You may at any time ask opponent how many strokes he has taken. If he gives wrong information and doesn't correct it before your next shot, he loses hole.

Penalty is disqualification if you and your opponent agree to waive any rule or penalty.

Penalty for carrying more than 14-club limit is loss of one hole for each extra club. Maximum penalty: Two holes. In four-ball, penalty applies to the side.

You may practice on the course before a match.

In any dispute or doubt about your rights or how to proceed, you must make a claim before teeing off on next hole. You don't have option to play a second ball.

(For official references, consult The Rules of Golf.)

HOW CART PENALTIES APPLY

Motorized carts are so commonly used now it can reward you well to know the penalty, if any, that might apply when an incident involves your cart or your ball.

First thing to understand is that your cart and everything in it—the other player, all bags, clubs, clothing, etc.—are **your** equipment, like a caddie.

Most carts are shared with another player, so it pays to know which incurs a penalty. Here we cover shared carts, and term "cart" includes everything in it.

A shared cart is like a caddie carrying double. It is the equipment of the player whose ball is involved. **Exception:** When cart is in motion the player driving it incurs any penalty.

Most USGA rulings involve carts deflecting or running over a ball. **Keeping exception in mind,** and assuming partners are sharing same cart, note these:

When your ball strikes your cart: In singles match, you lose hole; in four-ball, you are disqualified for hole. In stroke play, two strokes penalty.

When your ball strikes opponent's cart; No penalty, either in match or stroke play (rub of the green).

When you drive over your ball: You are penalized one stroke and the ball must be replaced.

When you drive over partner's ball: The partner is penalized one stroke and the ball must be replaced.

When you drive over opponent's ball: Ball must be replaced. You are penalized one stroke, but not if it occurred during search for ball.

Tournament committees are urged to set rules for use of carts, especially when not all players use them.

WINTER RULES

There are no established "winter rules." When a club adopts a local rule for "winter rules" or "preferred lies," it should be spelled out in detail by the committee. Without specifying what the rules allow, it's meaningless to post a notice: "Winter Rules Today."

USGA suggests the following rule as appropriate when adverse conditions make "winter rules" desirable, although it does not endorse and will not interpret it:

"A ball lying on a fairway may be lifted and cleaned, without penalty, and placed within six inches of where it originally lay, not nearer the hole, and so as to preserve as nearly as possible the stance required to play from the original lie. After the ball has been so placed, it is in play, and if it moves after the player has addressed it, the penalty shall be one stroke."

The rule may include the putting green if adverse conditions extend to it. It may be mandatory to move the ball from certain areas to protect them. Some clubs limit the rule to fairway of hole being played, to moving ball only with clubhead, and do not allow cleaning the ball, except as otherwise permitted.

The Rules of Golf make these observations:

"Winter rules" conflict with the fundamental principle of playing the ball as it lies. While sometimes adopted to protect course, the practical effect is just the opposite—permitting moving the ball to the best turf where divots taken damage the course further.

"Winter rules" tend generally to lower scores and handicaps, thus penalizing the players when competing against others who play under The Rules of Golf.

Extended use of "winter rules" also puts players at a disadvan-tage when required to play the ball as it lies. Scores made under "winter rules" may be accepted for handicapping if the committee considers that conditions warrant.

AMATEUR STATUS — USGA POLICY

An amateur golfer is defined by USGA rules as "one who plays the game solely as a non-remunerative or non-profit-making sport." Here are some ways you may lose amateur status without turning professional:

Accepting a prize worth more than $350 in merchandise.

Playing for prize money.

Accepting balls, clubs, clothes, etc., from a dealer in golf merchandise without paying market price, if your golf skill or reputation is associated with the product to help promote it.

Because of golf skill, accepting membership or privileges in a golf club, unless purely honorary.

Any conduct detrimental to golf, including gambling.

Amateur status is not affected by (1) mere statements of intention to turn pro, or (2) accepting expenses not related to golf ability, such as to play in a tournament staged by a business firm for its client.

HOLE-IN-ONE PRIZE—Hole-in-one contests, clubs or funds are covered by the $350 value prize restriction.

An amateur may accept up to $350 from a hole-in-one insurance club, which many clubs operate, in a gift certificate for merchandise or to cover related bar charges, but not for dues, restaurant or other charges.

Application for reinstatement of amateur status may be made to USGA. Probationary period of two years is normally imposed before reinstatement.

USGA will answer any question of doubt about amateur status. For complete information, read "Rules of Amateur Status" in The Rules of Golf, available in golf shops or from USGA, Far Hills, NJ 07931.

USGA POLICY ON GAMBLING

The definition of an amateur golfer provides that an amateur is one who plays the game as a non-remunerative sport. When gambling motives are introduced, problems can arise which threaten the integrity of the game.

The USGA does not object to participation in wagering among golfers or teams of golfers when participation in the wagering is limited to the players, the players may only wager on themselves or their teams, the sole source of all money won is advanced by the players and the primary purpose is the playing of the game for enjoyment.

The distinction between playing for prize money and gambling is essential to the validity of the Rules of Amateur Status. The following constitute golf wagering and not playing for prize money: 1. Participation in wagering among individual golfers. 2. Participation in wagering among teams.

Organized amateur events open to the general golfing public and designed and promoted to create cash prizes are not approved by the USGA. Golfers participating in such events without irrevocably waiving their right to cash prizes are deemed by the USGA to be playing for prize money.

The USGA is opposed to and urges its member clubs, all golf associations and all other sponsors of competitions to prohibit types of gambling such as: (1) Calcuttas, (2) other auction pools, (3) pari-mutuels and (4) any other form of gambling organized for general participation or permitting participants to bet on someone other than themselves or their teams.

It may deny amateur status, entry in USGA Championships and membership on USGA teams for international competitions to players whose activities in connection with golf gambling, whether organized or individual, are considered by the USGA to be contrary to the best interests of golf.

HANDICAPPING SYSTEMS

UNITED STATES GOLF ASSOCIATION

The USGA Handicap System is used by virtually all clubs and golf associations. The official handicap is computed by taking the lowest 10 of your last 20 scores, totaling differentials between your scores and course rating, and applying it to USGA Handicap Differential Chart.

Equitable Stroke Control

For handicap purposes only, the USGA in 1973 installed Equitable Stroke Control as a means of estimating scores for incompleted holes and reducing scores on "bad" holes. It put these limits on hole scores:

Plus or Scratch Handicap—One over par on any hole.

Handicaps 1-18—Two over par on number of holes equal to handicap; one over par on balance of holes.

Handicaps 19-36—Three over par on as many holes as handicap exceeds 18; two over on remainder.

Handicaps 37-40—Four over par on as many holes as handicap exceeds 36; three over on remainder.

Enter score for incompleted, or pickup, holes in accordance with above formula, putting X beside the score.

Handicap Allowances

On Jan. 1, 1978, USGA set new handicap allowances in multiball events designed to put teams on more equal footing:
Four-ball (better-ball) match play: Full handicap.
Four-ball stroke play: 90% of handicap.
Best-ball-of-four stroke play: 80% of handicap.
Two-best-balls-of-four play: 90% of handicap.

CALLAWAY

The Callaway Handicap System was originated and is copyrighted by Lionel F. Callaway of Pinehurst, N.C. It's useful for handicapping when many entrants in a tournament lack official handicaps.

The handicap is computed after the score is turned in. Using Callaway Chart, the player is allowed to deduct all or half of his scores on his worst holes up to six, depending on his actual score and under certain limitations, which are:

1—No hole may be scored at more than twice its par; 2—Half strokes count as a whole; 3—The 17th and 18th holes are never deducted; 4—As an equalizer, the handicap is adjusted up or down, up to two strokes, when the player's score does not fall in middle of a five-stroke range used for determining amount of handicap.

This table shows number of worst holes to deduct:

Score	Deduct	Score	Deduct	Score	Deduct
Par-75	½	91-95	2½	111-115	4½
76-80	1	96-100	3	116-120	5
81-85	1½	101-105	3½	121-125	5½
86-90	2	106-110	4	126-130	6

PEORIA

After all players in a tournament have teed off, select six holes—two par 3's, two par 4's and two par 5's. At the finish, total the player's scores for the six holes, multiply by three, subtract the course's par. Difference is player's handicap.

KINDS OF GOLF GAMES

BRIDGE GOLF

Two players play as team against two others. Stroke allowances are determined by the full difference in combined handicaps of the teams. Strokes apply to low ball of either team member and to team total (the bid) on holes where the strokes fall on the card.

Bidding begins after flip of coin on first tee. Winning team has choice of opening the bidding on either the nine odd or nine even numbered holes. Thereafter, on each tee the bidding team declares what its team total score will be on that hole, allowing for strokes on holes where they fall. The other team can bid a lower team total it expects to score or pass, allowing the other team to play for its bid. Rebidding can continue back and forth until one team decides it can bid no lower. Any bid can be doubled and redoubled. The team with the bid has the honor.

Scoring is by points, the teams having agreed beforehand on the money value of each point:

Making bid	1 plus point	Team low ball	2 points
Each stroke under bid	1 plus point	Team low total	2 points
		Birdie (gross)	1 point
Each stroke over bid	1 minus point	Greenie	1 point
(Double and redouble apply only to above points)		(Tee shot on green nearest cup on par 3)	

•

BINGLE-BANGLE-BUNGLE—Three points are scored on each hole: One to player whose ball reaches green first, one to player whose ball is nearest cup after all players are on green, and one who first sinks his putt.

KINDS OF GOLF GAMES (Cont.)

BOBS AND BIRDS—Bobs are points scored for tee shot on green and closest to pin on par-3 holes only; birds are points scored for birdies on any hole.

GREENIES—Closest tee shot on green on par-3 hole.

LOW AND HIGH BALL—Two points are scored on each hole; playing partners in a four-ball, low score wins a point, high score loses a point. Can also be played low ball-second low ball, or low ball-aggregate.

NASSAU—Points are scored for first nine, second nine and 18 holes, playing hole by hole.

PEPPERS—Partners win or lose peppers or points based on combination of their scores. If one makes par (or less), his score becomes first digit, his partner's the second. (E.g.: A makes par 4, B a 7. Score: 47.) If neither makes par, higher score becomes first digit. (E.g.: C makes 6, partner D an 8. Score: 86.) A and B win 39 peppers which cumulate hole by hole, through 18 holes.

POINT-QUOTA SYSTEM—Each player is given a point-quota, based on his handicap. Points are scored: bogey-1; par-2; birdie-4; eagle-8. Player whose point total for 18 holes most exceeds his point-quota (or comes closest if none exceeds it) wins. Find your point-quota opposite your handicap below:

HCP.	QTA.	HCP.	QTA.	HCP.	QTA.	HCP.	QTA.	HCP.	QTA.
1	35	7	29	13	23	19	17	25	11
2	34	8	28	14	22	20	16	26	10
3	33	9	27	15	21	21	15	27	9
4	32	10	26	16	20	22	14	28	8
5	31	11	25	17	19	23	13	29	7
6	30	12	24	18	18	24	12	30-40	6

ROUND ROBIN—Playing in a foursome, partners are changed every six holes. Thus, you play three six-hole matches with each of the players as a partner.

SPECKS—Player or side wins a speck for any of the following on each hole: Longest tee shot in fairway, first on green, closest to pin on approach, one-putt green, lowest score. Ties are split or cancelled. Players or side with most "specks" wins.

SYNDICATES—Sometimes called "skins." Match involves three or more playing together, and is by holes. Low score on a hole wins. If two tie, all tie. If you play cumulative syndicates, tied holes accumulate and go to next player to win.

TIN WHISTLE—On each hole, 1 point for one-over par, 3 points for par, 5 points for birdie. Partners, match play.

TIPS ON WAGERING

Not all golfers play the above games. If you do, you should of course try to play games that give you a fair chance. These suggestions may help:

Many games are won or lost on the first tee. Be cautious in making up sides. Don't over-estimate your own ability or under-estimate that of the others.

Wager modestly, no more than you are prepared to lose. This lessens your chances of "choking."

Don't make extra or press wagers when you are behind unless you feel you are playing well, but are losing only because you had bad breaks or your opponent had lucky ones.

On unusual wagers which involve an achievement, such as parring a hole, reaching a green or clearing an obstacle, try to make the wager that your opponent CAN'T do it rather than that you CAN.

If you play a steady, even game, don't play games which require spectacular holes to win. These are more often won by poorer golfers who get occasional pars and birdies.

KINDS OF SIDES AND MATCHES

Listed below are official terms for sides and matches which in some cases differ from those commonly used:

SIDE—One player or two or more who are partners.

SINGLES MATCH—One player against another.

TWOSOME—Same as Singles Match. (Commonly used term for two persons playing together.)

THREESOME—One player against two, with each side playing only one ball. (Commonly used term for three persons playing together.)

FOURSOME—Two players against two, each side playing one ball. Commonly called Scotch foursome. Partners may alternate driving, then alternate shots into the hole. Or, after deciding who will drive on No. 1, partners may alternate every stroke until they hole out on No. 18.

Two variations are more commonly played in the U.S.:

1. Selected Drives: Both partners drive, then select ball with which to complete the hole with alternate shots.

2. Pinehurst: Both partners drive, play each other's ball for the second stroke, then decide with which ball to hole out with alternate shots.

(Commonly used term for four persons playing together.)

THREE-BALL—Three play against one another, each playing his own ball. (Sometimes called round-robin.)

BEST BALL—One plays his ball against the better score (by holes) of two players or the best score of three players. (Commonly used term for a four-ball match.)

FOUR-BALL—Two partners play own ball, but only better score on each hole counts. (Commonly called best-ball or better ball of pairs.)

KINDS OF CLUB EVENTS

(List omits club championships of various obvious kinds.)

BEAT THE PRO TOURNAMENT — Using full handicap, members turn in net score for 18 holes. Those whose net is lower than gross score made by club professional win prizes.

BLIND BOGEY TOURNAMENT — When signing up the player chooses a handicap which he feels will assure a net score between 70 and 80. After play is completed, the committee puts numbers 70 to 80 in a hat and draws the winning number. The player whose net score is closest to that number wins.

CLASS TOURNAMENT — Divide field into four classes, A, B, C and D, based on handicap. Winners in each class are players with lowest net score. Ideally classes should be determined by dividing entrants or membership into four groups of approximately equal number.

FIELD DAY — Popular on opening and closing days of golf season, followed by dinner and golf movies. Some unusual prizes, such as hams and turkeys, awarded for a variety of events. Some examples: Low net, low gross, best comeback on back nine, longest drives, longest putts, best front and back nines. Tee shot within 12-foot circle on one or more par-3 holes wins ball.

FLAG TOURNAMENT — Popular on Decoration Day or Fourth of July. Each player is given small flag on stick. He sticks it in ground with his name on it where his ball lies after he has taken the number of strokes which equal par plus his handicap. The player who carries his flag farthest around the course (going extra holes if necessary) wins.

MINIATURE CHAMPIONSHIP — Same as regular club championship, with qualifying round and match-play pairings, except that matches are 9 instead of 18 holes. Four play together. Winners on front 9 play each other on back 9.

KINDS OF CLUB EVENTS (Cont.)

NO ALIBI TOURNAMENT — Instead of deducting his handicap, a player is allowed to replay a specified number of bad shots during the round. Some tournaments allow replay of as many shots as equal three-fourths of a player's handicap.

PAR COMPETITION — Using his handicap strokes where they fall on the card, contestant plays a match against par, hole by hole. One who makes best showing wins.

POINT TOURNAMENT — A player is awarded 4 points for each birdie he scores, 2 for each par, and 1 for each bogey. Allow full handicap strokes where they fall on card. Player with most points for 18 holes wins. Also played by teams.

RINGER TOURNAMENT — Each player or side plays two rounds. From the two cards the player or side selects better score on each hole. Lowest score for the selected 18 holes wins. Allow handicaps. Ideal for a weekend.

STRING TOURNAMENT — Player is given a piece of string in place of handicap strokes, measuring a foot of string for each handicap stroke. The player may move ball by hand to a more favorable spot at any time, measuring the distance moved with the string and cutting off the length used, until the string is used up. You may even use string to advance ball into hole or out of hazard without counting a stroke.

THROW-OUT TOURNAMENT — Before player turns in score, he is allowed to deduct one or more worst holes. Can also be played by teams. (Also called "Kickers.")

TEAM EVENTS

DERBY — Entrants are paired in groups of four, each group having one low, two medium and one high handicap player. On each hole the group enters on the card the lowest score of the group, deducting handicap strokes. (Sometimes called "best-ball of foursome.")

KINDS OF CLUB EVENTS (Cont.)

MIXED FOURSOMES — Man and woman comprise team. Popular on Sundays and holidays, particularly in Scotch foursomes, partners alternating strokes using one ball.

PRO-AM — Best player in group teams up as a "pro" with each of the others. Play is four-ball. Select better score of "pro" and "amateur" partner on each hole. Low 18-hole score wins.

SCRAMBLE — Play is in teams of four with comparable handicaps. All drive. Best ball is selected for second shot. Each player hits a ball from spot of selected drive. Again best ball is selected and all players hit a third shot from that spot. Continue this way to green and until ball is holed. Low score for 18 holes wins. No handicap allowance.

TWO-MAN TEAM — Better score of two partners counts on each hole. Match or stroke play, with or without handicap.

DOUBLE BEST-BALL — Like Derby. Score total of both lowest and second lowest net scores of foursome on each hole.

SEASON-LONG EVENTS

LADDER TOURNAMENT — Players are listed in order of handicap at start of season. Player may challenge any of three immediately above him to 18-hole match. If he wins, they exchange places. If he loses, he gives winner a new ball and may not challenge again until he has defended his own position against a challenge. Player at top at end of season wins.

RINGER TOURNAMENT — Contestant posts lowest score he makes on each hole during season. At end of season, one with lowest 18-hole score wins.

ROUND-ROBIN — Each entrant plays every other once at match play. Allowing for one match a week, it takes seven weeks to complete a cycle with eight competitors in a flight. Winner may be decided either by most matches won or highest total of "ups" by which player defeated his seven opponents, playing out all 18 holes in every match.

KINDS OF LEAGUES

MEN'S SUNDAY DERBY LEAGUE. A notice on the bulletin board will turn up names of players interested. When 20 or more sign up, league play starts. Five or six tee off times are reserved. Group is divided into classes: A - players - (up to 9), B - (10-15), C - (16-21), D - (22 or over). Names of those playing are put on slips and divided into classes. Foursomes are made up by drawing one A, one B, one C and one D player. Play is best ball of foursomes, using full handicaps. Each team plays every other team. Score is kept by front and back nines. Thus a team with a 6 and 2 means they shot six under on the front nine, 2 under on back. Team with highest score wins. Simultaneously, each player plays against a quota, using one point for a bogey, two for a par and four for a birdie. Quota is 36 minus handicap. If a player fails to make his quota, he pays in $1 into pot for season prizes.

MIXED 9-HOLE TWILIGHT LEAGUE. League is formed at start of Daylight Saving. League meets every Thursday or Friday, first foursome teeing off at 4:00. Every week play is different; Mixed Scotch Foursomes, Pinehurst, Scramble, String or Flag (See Kinds of Club Events). Sometimes couples are split up and paired with others by lot. When play is by couples, only one quarter of combined handicap is used. Each couple pays $2 into pot every week. Pot is used to buy a dozen balls every week which are given as prizes. Twelve lowest scorers each win a ball. Couples usually stay for dinner. Remainder of pot is used for prizes and refreshments at a final tournament. As season draws to a close, shotgun starts are used so all players finish before dark.

INDUSTRIAL LEAGUES. Run by companies after work, weekly 9-hole matches. Prizes at end for best won-lost record.

GENERAL
INFORMATION

HOW TO BUY CLUBS THAT FIT YOU

There's more to buying golf clubs than picking a set that "feels good." Clubs must be fitted to suit your swing, stance, build, strength, age and taste.

Even though individual sets may be matched, different sets have varying characteristics as to overall weight, weight distribution, length and flex of shaft, shape and lie of clubhead, thickness and type of grip — all in different combinations.

How weight is distributed between head and shaft determines swing weight, which affects how heavy the club will seem when you swing it. Swingweights usually range from D1 to D5 for men and C4 to C7 for women. The faster you swing, the lighter swingweight you'll want.

Shafts come in different flexes, from very stiff to whippy, commonly marked X, S, R, A and for ladies L. What flex will suit you will depend primarily on factors of age, strength, build and how fast you swing.

Consider also new graphite and stainless steel shafts which are claimed to add distance to your shots.

Usually, the stronger golfer needs a heavy club with stiff shaft, whereas a slight person does better with a light club on flexible shaft, as do those over 50. The slow, deliberate swinger needs a whippy shaft; the fast swinger a stiffer one.

A heavier club won't necessarily give you more power. It will in fact reduce power if it robs you of lashing hand action. Speed of clubhead is just as important as weight, so that you might get more distance from a lighter club with a stiff shaft which will permit faster striking speed.

For these reasons, only an experienced golf professional can fit you properly. So if you want clubs that are best for YOU, have your pro study your swing and fit you with the right clubs.

HOW TO TAKE CARE OF YOUR GEAR

Take good care of your golf equipment. Top quality clubs, shoes and bags are costly to replace. Not only will good care make your gear last longer and give you more for your money, but you will play better and get more enjoyment out of the game. Storing clubs at your Pro Shop will help because storage fees include cleaning after each round. Some other tips you can use:

WOODS — Keep head covers on all the time unless they are wet. Before storing clubs, remove wet head covers and wipe heads dry. Do not replace head covers until thoroughly dry. Wipe heads clean after each round.

IRONS — Keep clubface clean and grooves free of dirt for better backspin and control. Wash with soap and water. Use of harsh brush, steel wool or abrasive may damage chrome.

GRIPS — To revive tacky feel to leather grips, apply light coat of caster oil or leather conditioner. Wash rubber grips with suds and water.

BAG — Use bag of ample size to protect grips and shafts. Treat leather bag twice a year with leather conditioner. Replace worn strap. Don't sit on bag. Some golfers use plastic tubes to protect grips and spread clubs evenly.

SHOES — Remove grass and dirt from spikes and soles after every round. Leather will crack and stiffen, and rubber deteriorates, when subject to wide variations in temperature, such as occurs in car trunk. Polish and treat with leather conditioner. Use shoe trees to keep shape. Keep spikes tight.

GENERAL TIPS: Moisture is wood clubs worst enemy. Keep them in dry place, but away from heat. Do not place any weight on them, as you might in car trunk. Leaning on or pounding club on ground may cause error in face alignment. Store glove in plastic bag to keep soft and pliable.

PLAYING ETIQUETTE

Golf is a game in which good manners and consideration of others are essential. Considerate golfers and spectators follow these cardinal rules:

Don't move, talk, make noise or otherwise disturb a player about to make a stroke. Don't stand close to a player who is addressing the ball, or on a line behind the ball where he can see you. Don't offer unsolicited advice or instruction.

Replace divots. Repair ball and spike marks on the green. Smooth footprints when leaving a bunker.

Don't drop your bag, pull a golf cart or drive a golf car on the green. Avoid damaging the green by dropping the flagstick or standing close to the cup. Don't step on the line of anyone's putt. Don't stand so that your shadow falls on another's line of putt. Leave the green immediately after completing the hole. Mark your score **after** leaving green.

Delay hitting until those ahead are well out of range.

If there is a clear hole open ahead, invite the match behind to play through. Do the same when looking for a lost ball.

Play without undue delay. Be prepared to play when your turn comes. This means studying your next shot and deciding the club you will use as you approach your ball or wait for the others to play. When you have the honor on the tee, don't waste time washing your ball or engaging in idle conversation. It's a good idea also to carry a spare ball in your pocket for the time when you might have to play a second or provisional ball.

Allow the player whose ball is the farthest from the hole to play first. However, to save time in a friendly game you sometimes might play out of turn if others farther away are not ready. You might also concede putts "within the leather," although this is not permitted in competition.

ETIQUETTE FOR GUESTS

Most golfers know what's expected of them at their own club. But many, particularly if they are not private club members, wonder what's the proper thing to do when they're guests at a club. Here are a few suggestions:

Don't be late. Know exactly what time you are expected, where to meet — and be on time. If it's not obvious, ask whether you should come dressed for play.

Most important to consider when you're a guest is your relationship with your host. If you are a customer (or a prospective one), your host will take care of everything. You may offer to pay for the cart or caddie and tip the locker man, but not the green fee. If your club has a reciprocal arrangement, you may try to sign the tab for a round of drinks. If not, forget it, because most clubs won't take cash.

If your host is a friend, you should offer to pay for the cart or caddie and tip the locker man. You can also offer to pay the green fee and your share of any meals, but do it privately. And you can sign for a round of drinks or reimburse him. If your host insists on taking care of everything, let him, but remember, you should return the courtesy promptly by entertaining him at your own club.

Make sure you know what your handicap is. Let your host handle any decisions about betting in your foursome.

Winners usually buy the first round of drinks. So if you win, you should offer to buy. When your host is buying, don't wear out your welcome by lingering too long at the 19th—if you want to be invited back. Offer to leave after a reasonable time; don't make your host have to suggest it's time to go.

As soon as possible, invite your host to play at your club, or entertain him in some other way. When you do, you should handle the expenses the same way he did at his club.

HOW TO SPEED UP PLAY

Slow play steals much of the enjoyment expected from golf. To help speed up play, the USGA urges you in stroke play to putt continuously until you hole out unless you might step in another player's line, in which case you should mark. This minimizes ball marking and loss of time.

Check yourself to see if you are unconciously doing these things which slow up play and can be avoided.

Do you fail to know—and are you unprepared—when it is your turn to play?

While others are playing their shot, do you neglect to size up yours and decide what club to use?

With a caddie carrying double, when you go in another direction from the player sharing the caddie, do you neglect to take several clubs with you?

Do you forget to carry a second ball in your pocket?

Do you fail to invite players to go through when there's an open hole ahead or you are looking for a ball?

Do you distract and delay others by idle chatter?

Do you try to give others a lesson during a round?

Do you fail to take extra clubs with you when you leave the area of a golf cart to play a shot?

Are you over-careful and time-consuming in trying to figure out the line of a putt from several angles?

Do you fail to study your putt and get yourself ready while others are putting?

Do you re-try putts while others are waiting?

Do you wait until after holing out to count your strokes?

Do you do your score-keeping on the putting green?

If you do these things to delay your group or others behind you, you may deserve the penalty for undue delay—loss of hole in match play or two strokes in stroke play (Rule 37-7).

EARMARKS OF A DUFFER

A duffer does more than play poor golf. He gives himself away by some of the things he does or fails to do that are typical of beginners — although many experienced players are guilty and may be put in this class.

Some things duffers do violate the rules: some just violate etiquette. All are avoidable. If your answer is "Yes," to most of these questions, you rate in the duffer class:

ON THE TEE, do you: Tee up in front of the markers, even just a little? Drive before group ahead is out of range?

THROUGH THE GREEN, do you: Walk ahead of others in your group and risk being hit? Stand too close to one about to play a stroke? Press the grass behind the ball down with your foot or club? Forget to count strokes when you whiff or lose a ball? Pull up grass or weeds when in the rough or break off branches that obstruct your swing?

IN A BUNKER, do you: Leave footprints unraked? Touch the sand with the club when addressing the ball?

ON THE GREEN, do you: Change to a new "putting ball"? Place your marker in front, instead of behind the ball? Leave your ball in the cup after holing out when others still have to putt? Step on another's line of putt? Press down with your putter or foot to smooth your line? Lean on your putter, scuff the green with your spikes, fail to repair your ball mark? After putting out, do you stay on the green to count strokes or mark the score?

IF YOU PLAY LIKE A DUFFER, don't despair. Many good golfers began as duffers. Lessons and practice are the surest way out of dufferdom. A novel approach is offered by Bogey Breakers, who teach you by mail how to play smarter and avoid the dumb shots. For free trial membership, write to Bogey Breakers, P.O. Box 4065, Washington, D.C. 20015.

YOUR LEGAL RIGHTS AND RISKS

Whether you're a golfer or spectator, you assume the obvious and ordinary risks you'll normally encounter on a golf course.

There's a hazard of a freak shot by an expert or a poor one by a duffer. About the only time a golfer might recover for injuries is when he was within the other player's range when struck.

Yelling "Fore" won't necessarily absolve a player of blame but it may be considered a mitigating factor. Courts agree that a warning shout is proper, but it should be made before shooting, otherwise it might cause someone to move into the path of the ball.

Failure to yell "Fore" may not make you liable if the person who was injured was aware that you were about to shoot and had an opportunity to get out of the way of your shot.

Ordinarily, you are required to warn only those persons in direct line of fire, not those on your flanks. Freak shots, such as balls bouncing off trees or rocks, or those shanked or otherwise hit at unusual angles, are usually not considered your fault.

On the other hand, a Pennsylvania court held that a golfer may be held responsible for injury caused when a driver slipped out of his hands because he failed to wipe them and struck one of his foursome sitting in a golf cart 20 feet behind him.

An Oklahoma court said it's well known that not every shot goes where it's intended; if such were the case, every player would be perfect and the whole pleasure of the sport would be lost.

A jury in Atlantic City awarded $7,500 to a caddie who was struck by a ball and partially lost his sight. The boy was about 75 yards from the tee, to one side. The decision hinged on the fact that the player knew the caddie wasn't watching and did not yell "Fore" until after he had hit the ball.

FIRST AID ON THE COURSE

ARTIFICIAL RESPIRATION — If victim is not breathing apply mouth-to-mouth breathing AT ONCE. Lay victim on back. Clear mouth and throat. Tilt head back. Pull chin up. Place mouth over victim's, pinch victim's nostrils, take deep breath, blow hard enough to make victim's chest rise. Remove mouth, let victim's chest fall. Repeat at rate of 12 breaths a minute (20 for children) until victim breathes naturally.

BLEEDING — Do not wash wound. Press down on bleeding point, wrap with handkerchief, piece of shirt, towel, etc. If bleeding won't stop, apply pressure above wound, at pressure points. If a tourniquet is used, it should be loosened only by a doctor.

BROKEN BONE — Whether simple or compound. DON'T move victim. Send for doctor. Make victim lie still.

FAINTING — Have victim sit with head between knees or lie down with head lower than feet. Sprinkle water on face. Don't give stimulant. Send for doctor.

HEART ATTACK — Send for doctor. Make victim comfortable. Loosen tight clothing. Maintain body temperature. DON'T let victim move. DON'T give stimulant. Suggest slow, deep breaths. Give medication if victim has it available.

INSECT BITES — Remove stinger if present. Apply mud or wet cloth. If victim faints, is nauseous or has weak pulse, send for doctor. Keep victim still with head lower than heart, maintain body temperature.

LIGHTNING — If victim is not breathing, apply mouth-to-mouth breathing AT ONCE. Send for doctor. Make victim comfortable. Maintain body temperature.

SUN STROKE — Lay victim on back in shade with head slightly elevated. Cool head and body with water. Rub arms and legs toward heart. Send for doctor.

(Reviewed by Montgomery County, Md., Chapter, Red Cross)

LIGHTNING SAFETY

Lightning causes many deaths and injuries on golf courses. Here are some precautions recommended:

Delay starting, or call off, a match before an electrical storm is near enough to be hazardous. If you are caught on the course, seek shelter in a building and stay away from fireplaces, stoves and other metal objects.

Choose shelter in this order: 1—Large metal or metal-frame building; 2—Buildings protected against lightning; 3—Large unprotected building; 4—Small building.

If you must remain outdoors, keep away from: Small exposed shelter, isolated tree, wire fence, hilltop, open space. Lightning has also been known to strike a golf cart.

Seek shelter in a cave, depression, foot of hill, dense woods, grove of trees, or lie flat.

In tournament, heed siren warning to halt play.

HOW TO OPERATE A GOLF CART

Here are some suggestions for operating golf carts:

Make certain you know how to start and stop the cart, and test the brakes, before leaving the first tee.

Start the cart gradually. When you are in a moving cart, don't stand up, hang out, or carry a club. Don't drive recklessly. Observe course rules and direction signs.

Keep cart well away from player about to make a stroke so as not to disturb him. Lock brake when leaving cart.

Respect condition of turf. Avoid low areas when ground is soft. Don't spin wheels, drive on tees or apron of greens. Keep cart at least 20 feet from front of greens. Always leave cart on the side of or behind greens so following players can hit up with less waiting.

Drive straight up or down slopes, rather than along slopes, causing cart to tilt precariously. Avoid steep slopes.

HOW TO WATCH A TOURNAMENT

For spectators, golf has no equal in major sports. None can compare with golf for the opportunities it offers fans to virtually rub shoulders with their heroes and improve their own skills, while enjoying the competition and open air.

Aware of this, fans are flocking to golf tournaments in such increasing numbers that special care must be taken to handle the crowds in the interest of both players and spectators. Ropes to guide spectators are now common at major events.

At any tournament, these tips may be helpful:

Check for program, with course diagram, and pairings.

If you like to just watch all of the golfers, sit behind a green or tee. A folding chair will come in handy.

If you like to walk, observe the ropes and other crowd controls. Walk the course in reverse, starting at the 18th hole, so that you won't miss seeing the early starters.

Find vantage points where you might watch both putting and driving without too much moving around. When watching putts, do not leave the green area until all players have holed out. If you want to be sure to see a particular player drive, station yourself at the tee well ahead of time.

To keep up with progress of the competition, keep a close eye on "leader" boards spotted on the course.

To improve your own game, watch the better players hit the shots you're having the most trouble with. Watch how they stand, address the ball, start their swing, pivot, hit, follow through. Storing a mental image of all or part of the swing and trying to imitate it later can help you with your problems.

Don't disturb the players or disrupt their concentration. Don't move or talk when a shot is being played near you. Get autographs before or after the round. If you bring a camera, you will have to check it at the gate on the PGA Tour.

GLOSSARY OF GOLF TERMS

ACE—A hole played in one stroke. Hole-in-one.

ADDRESS—Position when a player has taken his stance preparatory to hitting ball.

ALBATROSS—Hole score three strokes under par. Double eagle.

APPROACH—Shot to green; area in front of green.

APRON—Area immediately bordering green, generally mowed about halfway between green and fairway height.

AWAY—Ball farthest from hole and to be played next.

BACKSPIN—Backward spin of ball after being struck.

BALL—To meet USGA specifications, a golf ball must not be smaller than 1.68 inches in diameter, weigh not more than 1.62 ounces and travel not faster than 255 feet per second or more than 280 yards when tested at 75 degrees temperature on USGA apparatus. British rules permit ball to be as small as 1.62 inches in diameter, with same weight as U.S. ball.

BANANA BALL—Slice; shot that starts left and fades right. (From right to left for left-handed player.)

BEST-BALL—Term commonly used for four-ball play.

BINGLE-BANGLE-BUNGLE—(See Kinds of Golf Games.)

BIRDIE—Hole score one stroke under par.

BISQUE—Handicap stroke that may be taken on any hole at option of recipient before teeing off on next hole.

BLIND BOGEY—Competition in which players, before teeing off, estimate handicaps required to net them scores between 70 and 80. A "blind" figure in this range is then selected and player with closest net is declared winner.

BLIND HOLE—One on which green is hidden from view and cannot be seen when approaching it.

BOGEY—In U.S., commonly refers to score of one above par on a hole. In other countries, it refers to score average person should be able to make on a hole, with par and bogey being the same on some easier holes.

BRASSIE—Old name for No. 2 wood.

BUNKER—A hazard consisting of depression covered with sand. A sandtrap, or trap.

CADDIE—Carries a player's bag and may give advice.

CHIP SHOT—Short approach shot of low trajectory.

COURSE RATING—A rating in strokes of the playing difficulty of a course. Rating is done by an association to provide the basis for uniform handicapping irrespective of difficulty.

CUT SHOT—Outside-in swing at ball.

DIVOT—Piece of sod that is cut away by club.

DOG-LEG—Hole where fairway turns to left or right.

DORMIE—When a player or side in match play is as many holes up as remain to be played.

DOWN—When a side is behind in a match, indicated by number of holes. Opposite of up, for ahead.

DUCK HOOK—Right-to-left curving shot in which ball veers or hooks and drops sharply. (Left to right for left-hander.)

DUFFER—Unskilled golfer; dub; hacker.

EAGLE—Hole score two strokes under par.

EXPLOSION—Sandtrap shot in which clubface is brought into and through sand under ball; blast.

FAIRWAY—Closely mowed area between tee and green.

FLUSH—To hit ball with full swing precisely on clubface.

FORE—Warning cry to any and all persons who are within range of a shot. Request for silence and immobility. Its use has been ruled in courts as mitigating the liability of golfer whose ball strikes and injures a person.

FOUR-BALL—Competition in which two partners use only the better of their scores on each hole. (Commonly called Best-Ball.)

FOURSOME—A colloquialism for four golfers playing together. (Also: Threesome for three players; twosome for two.)(See Kinds of Sides and Matches.)

FROG-HAIR—Short grass bordering edge of green.

GRAIN—The lie of the grass on a putting green.

GREENIES—A game. (See Kinds of Golf Games.)

GROSS SCORE—Score before handicap is deducted.

HAZARD—A ditch, stream, lake or bunker (sandtrap).

HOLE HIGH—A long shot come to rest even with the hole.

HONOR—Right to drive or play first, determined by lowest score on preceding hole, or by other means on first tee.

LIE—Position of ball on ground. Also angle between clubhead and shaft.

LINKS—A seaside golf course.

LIP—Edge of hole or front edge of bunker.

MATCH PLAY—Two-sided competition by holes. Match ends when one side is ahead by more holes than there are left.

MEDAL PLAY—(See Stroke Play).

MEDALIST—Competitor with lowest qualifying score preceding match play.

MULLIGAN—Second ball sometimes allowed after poor tee shot, usually on first tee. Not permitted under rules.

NASSAU—A competition in which three points are scored, one for each nine and for the 18 holes. Believed to have originated at Nassau (N.Y.) CC.

NET—Score after handicap is deducted.

OUT-OF-BOUNDS—Ground on which play is prohibited.

PAR—Score an expert golfer would make for a hole under ordinary weather conditions allowing two putts per hole.

PITCH SHOT—Short approach shot of high trajectory which travels very little after it falls to the turf.

PRESS—(1) Effort to apply more than normal power and hope for better than normal results from a shot; (2) An extra bet, usually on last few holes or on second nine of a Nassau wager for amount loser lost on first nine.

90

PUNCH SHOT—A low shot executed by punching club down at the ball. Usually played to green into heavy wind.

RINGER TOURNAMENT—(see Kinds of Club Events.)

ROUGH—Area of long grass not maintained as fairway.

ROUND-ROBIN—Tournament in which every player meets every other player one time.

RUB OF THE GREEN—This occurs when a ball in motion is stopped or deflected by an outside agency.

SCRATCH PLAYER—One whose handicap is zero.

SCOTCH FOURSOME—A common term for competition in which two partners play one ball, alternating strokes.

SHANK—When ball flies off neck or hosel of club.

SKY—To hit ball very high with little distance.

SNAKE—Long putt with several "borrows."

STROKE PLAY—Competition in which total of the hole by hole score determines the result. Medal play.

STYMIE—When opponent's ball is on the line of a player's putt in match play. Disallowed in early Fifties.

SUDDEN DEATH—When a match is tied after playing last hole, additional holes played until one player wins.

SWEET SPOT—Most effective hitting spot on club face.

SWINGWEIGHT—Indicates weight distribution between shaft/club head: overall balance factor. D2, C1, etc.

TEXAS WEDGE—A putter when used from chipping distance or out of a sandtrap.

TEE—Area two club lengths behind and between tee markers on which to tee ball for drive. Also a peg or other object to hold ball off the ground for tee shot.

TOE—Tip or end of clubhead.

WAGGLE—Short swings of the clubhead in the process of addressing the ball prior to striking it.

WHIFF—When player's stroke misses ball completely.

GOLFING LOG

Date _____ Course _____ Weather _____

PLAYER (1) _____ HANDICAP _____
PLAYER (2) _____ HANDICAP _____
PLAYER (3) _____ HANDICAP _____
PLAYER (4) _____ HANDICAP _____

HOLE	PAR	(1)	(2)	(3)	(4)	+/−
1						
2						
3						
4						
5						
6						
7						
8						
9						
TOTAL OUT						
10						
11						
12						
13						
14						
15						
16						
17						
18						
TOTAL IN						
TOTAL IN-OUT						
LESS HANDICAP						

GOLFING LOG

Date _____ Course _____ Weather _____

PLAYER (1) _____ HANDICAP _____
PLAYER (2) _____ HANDICAP _____
PLAYER (3) _____ HANDICAP _____
PLAYER (4) _____ HANDICAP _____

HOLE	PAR	(1)	(2)	(3)	(4)	+/−
1						
2						
3						
4						
5						
6						
7						
8						
9						
TOTAL OUT						
10						
11						
12						
13						
14						
15						
16						
17						
18						
TOTAL IN						
TOTAL IN-OUT						
LESS HANDICAP						

GOLFING LOG

Date _____ Course _____ Weather _____

PLAYER (1) _____ HANDICAP _____
PLAYER (2) _____ HANDICAP _____
PLAYER (3) _____ HANDICAP _____
PLAYER (4) _____ HANDICAP _____

HOLE	PAR	(1)	(2)	(3)	(4)	+/−
1						
2						
3						
4						
5						
6						
7						
8						
9						
TOTAL OUT						
10						
11						
12						
13						
14						
15						
16						
17						
18						
TOTAL IN						
TOTAL IN-OUT						
LESS HANDICAP						

Golf scorecard — three identical blank scoring panels.

Panel 1

Date _____ Course _____ Weather _____

PLAYER (1) _____ HANDICAP _____
PLAYER (2) _____ HANDICAP _____
PLAYER (3) _____ HANDICAP _____
PLAYER (4) _____ HANDICAP _____

HOLE	PAR	(1)	(2)	(3)	(4)	+|
1						
2						
3						
4						
5						
6						
7						
8						
9						
TOTAL OUT						
10						
11						
12						
13						
14						
15						
16						
17						
18						
TOTAL IN						
TOTAL IN-OUT						
LESS HANDICAP						
NET SCORE						

Panel 2

Date _____ Course _____ Weather _____

PLAYER (1) _____ HANDICAP _____
PLAYER (2) _____ HANDICAP _____
PLAYER (3) _____ HANDICAP _____
PLAYER (4) _____ HANDICAP _____

HOLE	PAR	(1)	(2)	(3)	(4)	+|
1						
2						
3						
4						
5						
6						
7						
8						
9						
TOTAL OUT						
10						
11						
12						
13						
14						
15						
16						
17						
18						
TOTAL IN						
TOTAL IN-OUT						
LESS HANDICAP						
NET SCORE						

Panel 3

Date _____ Course _____ Weather _____

PLAYER (1) _____ HANDICAP _____
PLAYER (2) _____ HANDICAP _____
PLAYER (3) _____ HANDICAP _____
PLAYER (4) _____ HANDICAP _____

HOLE	PAR	(1)	(2)	(3)	(4)	+|
1						
2						
3						
4						
5						
6						
7						
8						
9						
TOTAL OUT						
10						
11						
12						
13						
14						
15						
16						
17						
18						
TOTAL IN						
TOTAL IN-OUT						
LESS HANDICAP						
NET SCORE						

GOLFING LOG

Date	Course	Weather
PLAYER (1) _____		HANDICAP _____
PLAYER (2) _____		HANDICAP _____
PLAYER (3) _____		HANDICAP _____
PLAYER (4) _____		HANDICAP _____

HOLE	PAR	(1)	(2)	(3)	(4)	+ −
1						
2						
3						
4						
5						
6						
7						
8						
9						
TOTAL OUT						
10						
11						
12						
13						
14						
15						
16						
17						
18						
TOTAL IN						
TOTAL IN-OUT						
LESS HANDICAP						

GOLFING LOG

Date	Course	Weather
PLAYER (1) _____		HANDICAP _____
PLAYER (2) _____		HANDICAP _____
PLAYER (3) _____		HANDICAP _____
PLAYER (4) _____		HANDICAP _____

HOLE	PAR	(1)	(2)	(3)	(4)	+ −
1						
2						
3						
4						
5						
6						
7						
8						
9						
TOTAL OUT						
10						
11						
12						
13						
14						
15						
16						
17						
18						
TOTAL IN						
TOTAL IN-OUT						
LESS HANDICAP						

GOLFING LOG

Date	Course	Weather
PLAYER (1) _____		HANDICAP _____
PLAYER (2) _____		HANDICAP _____
PLAYER (3) _____		HANDICAP _____
PLAYER (4) _____		HANDICAP _____

HOLE	PAR	(1)	(2)	(3)	(4)	+ −
1						
2						
3						
4						
5						
6						
7						
8						
9						
TOTAL OUT						
10						
11						
12						
13						
14						
15						
16						
17						
18						
TOTAL IN						
TOTAL IN-OUT						
LESS HANDICAP						

Three identical golf scorecard forms appear on this page. Each has the following structure:

Date _____ Course _____ Weather _____

PLAYER (1) _____ HANDICAP _____
PLAYER (2) _____ HANDICAP _____
PLAYER (3) _____ HANDICAP _____
PLAYER (4) _____ HANDICAP _____

HOLE	PAR	(1)	(2)	(3)	(4)	+ −
1						
2						
3						
4						
5						
6						
7						
8						
9						
TOTAL OUT						
10						
11						
12						
13						
14						
15						
16						
17						
18						
TOTAL IN						
TOTAL IN-OUT						
LESS HANDICAP						
NET SCORE						

GOLFING LOG

Date _____ Course _____ Weather _____

PLAYER (1) _____ HANDICAP _____
PLAYER (2) _____ HANDICAP _____
PLAYER (3) _____ HANDICAP _____
PLAYER (4) _____ HANDICAP _____

HOLE	PAR	(1)	(2)	(3)	(4)	+/-
1						
2						
3						
4						
5						
6						
7						
8						
9						
TOTAL OUT						
10						
11						
12						
13						
14						
15						
16						
17						
18						
TOTAL IN						
TOTAL IN-OUT						
LESS HANDICAP						

GOLFING LOG

Date _____ Course _____ Weather _____

PLAYER (1) _____ HANDICAP _____
PLAYER (2) _____ HANDICAP _____
PLAYER (3) _____ HANDICAP _____
PLAYER (4) _____ HANDICAP _____

HOLE	PAR	(1)	(2)	(3)	(4)	+/-
1						
2						
3						
4						
5						
6						
7						
8						
9						
TOTAL OUT						
10						
11						
12						
13						
14						
15						
16						
17						
18						
TOTAL IN						
TOTAL IN-OUT						
LESS HANDICAP						

GOLFING LOG

Date _____ Course _____ Weather _____

PLAYER (1) _____ HANDICAP _____
PLAYER (2) _____ HANDICAP _____
PLAYER (3) _____ HANDICAP _____
PLAYER (4) _____ HANDICAP _____

HOLE	PAR	(1)	(2)	(3)	(4)	+/-
1						
2						
3						
4						
5						
6						
7						
8						
9						
TOTAL OUT						
10						
11						
12						
13						
14						
15						
16						
17						
18						
TOTAL IN						
TOTAL IN-OUT						
LESS HANDICAP						